Kiss Every Frog You Find: A Modern Girl's Quest to Find Her Prince

Kristin Tara McNamara

Maculated Press
San Luis Obispo

DEDICATION

To Mom, because she's mentioned a squillion times in this, to Yishai, who proved her wrong for loving me just the way I am, and to Mr. PleaseDon'tWriteAboutUs, for inspiring me to write this book.

CONTENTS

INTRODUCTION

I have had this book written in my head for years; whenever anyone would mention a terrible dating story, I'd always have one to counter it. It became something of a regular entertainment for friends when there was a lull at parties. I made friends by sharing them. It wasn't until a particularly confusing dating experience with someone I'm now very good friends with, that I finally sat down to really make a book. As I wrote them, I started to feel guilty.

I made a name for myself in the rock climbing world by posting stories on rock climbing websites about adventures gone bad. In a culture where there's pride in the ascent and the strength of the individual that made it, I was offering something different: a tangible account of what happens to the rest of us: an unabashed admission of my failure. Of course, it was my version of the story and that meant it was always someone else's fault.

I approached this book in the same way: these were trip reports about boys. It was almost always a crash and burn, but I learned along the way and the views were pretty spectacular. But it's hard for me to write stories about real people and real occurrences when it comes to love. If nothing else, most of us just muddle through life looking for the fairy tale or settle for something like it. Hitting that emotional scar can really run deep.

Moreover, as I wrote this book, the guy that inspired it kept begging me not to put our experience in it. When he did particularly stupid things, his first comment was always, "Please don't write about this!"

The key here is that I am feeling a little guilty about doing what I'm doing. What I'm doing is kind of mean, isn't it? Is this supposed to be a catalog of all the fools I've been through in the quest for love? No. It's supposed to be a funny collection of war stories. Lord knows I'm not perfect. We all have our stupid things we display and have to get over. And we all search for someone who's the same kind of crazy that we are and helps us come to find ourselves.

I believe healthy love is really all of a piece. One of my best friends Ellie recommended *Being in Love* by Osho that explains it very nicely: "Love should give you freedom; never settle for less." It's that ultimate freedom that makes you whole. The other person doesn't fill the holes you have - the other person facilitates you doing it yourself by motivating you to free yourself from your personal inner demons. Love is about dropping the insecurities and really being vulnerable - like a baby - and trusting that someone's going to take care of you and love you for who you are.

I think that's why I like dogs so much.

I think that's also why we love our families despite all the crazy shenanigans they pull. Because, when the chips are down, if we're lucky, we can go running home to Mom and Dad or Bro or Sis and be *vulnerable*.

And the key, I think, is not having expectations except that you can *be* with that person. You can exist and at the same time you can make mistakes. To people who love you, it doesn't matter.

I am searching for a man that allows me to do that. Just as most of those I write about (or don't write about) were and are doing the same. We are born into this world with trust and we build up defense mechanisms when we find out not everyone is out to keep us safe. This is not a parade of fools: its stories about how defense mechanisms work or don't work. Writing them, and thinking about the men in my past life, has shown me patterns of my own behavior that aren't the best. I hope you can appreciate that. Each of these guys had their own inner demons that didn't want to dance with mine - that's it.

And if you can't laugh with me because you see in these stories your own ineptitude - that's tragedy.

May you find and keep the love you deserve.

Remember, the princess rode off with prince charming only because she was willing to kiss a frog to get what she desired.

1 FOLLOW YOUR INSTINCTS

I used to have a policy in effect: if a guy asks me out, I promise to accept. The idea behind it was (a) I am a huge loser and in return for the compliment, I should at least give the person a chance and (b) I know how much courage it can take to ask someone out that you like and I will reward courage every time.

Friends sometimes told me it was cruel to accept dates from men I had no interest in, but not being of cruel heart, I disagree. The problem was, however, when a real lout comes along, it's not a reward he gets; it's enabling support from me.

This, you shall see, is a very bad thing for . . . me and all women to follow me.

When choosing boys to date, if you have a negative impression of him upon multiple meetings, you should probably not hook up with him.

Just saying.

Okay, so, Smarmy was my crazy roommate's lab partner. A good looking guy, he and I had some interesting intellectual discussions that were not about literature (which is really all I tended to get while in grad school, for obvious reasons) at parties, but there was something I couldn't put my finger on. I just always felt like he had the quiet confidence of a used car salesman, inspiring the grease-laden mistrust that comes along with it. Every time I would see him, he would make a bee-line for me and then spend the entire time insulting me. Boy, does that turn a chick on.

It was funny, too. When I saw him out of context, I wouldn't recognize him. He was a good looking guy in a very nondescript, generalized blonde-haired, blue-eyed way. He looked like pretty much every other student on campus and when he'd run into me my eyes would haze over until I worked it out, embarrassed. I'd see him (or someone I thought was a reasonable approximation of him) and avoid him because I could never be sure. I've yet to meet another person I couldn't recognize after having at least one conversation with. It was a gift of his, I suppose.

But, being persistent, he did what many men in my life have done: he wore me down. He kept telling my roommate how cute and cool I was, and when he found out about my "Won't Say No to a Date" doctrine, he invoked it. I wanted to give him a chance, so on a day that happened to be his birthday, I agreed to go over to his house to keep him company and watch a movie. And, if you are anywhere near my generation, you know what this means: it means dark rooms and boy hoping for action.

What can I say, it was his birthday!

I am a nice girl, and he begged me to come over – poor lonely guy in the beginning of grad school with no friends on his birthday. Oh, but don't get the wrong impression: we watched *Shrek 2*, which ended in wrestling and chaste kissing before I realized what was happening and hurried home.

As a result of this, we were officially dating, I suppose, but it happened shortly before Winter Break and there wasn't much advancement beyond this point when we both went our separate ways for the holidays. Not one for a break, he invites me to go on a ski weekend, and we would be staying at his married best friend's house an hour from the slopes in Sacramento. Normally I would not be into something so committing this early on, but I couldn't imagine what the harm was, so I agreed.

He picked me up at my house and my mom was just thrilled with him. She dragged him inside, showing him the house and tittering, "Oh, so cute. So polite! This one's a keeper!"

My mom is incredibly bad at keeping her cool with guests I bring home. I was so mortified I could barely look at him the whole drive to Sacramento.

We drove up to Sacramento to the friend's house and then went out for dinner. In a grand display of chivalry, taking my arm in his and opening the door for me, Smarmy took great care to be sure to give me the back seat with the most leg like a true gentleman. It was the first time in my life anyone had given me the consideration of Most Leg Room, and it was a great luxury: I mean, at five-foot-six - and most of it body - I am a towering giant in need of leg room.

His friends set us up on the living room fold-out couch. At this point, I haven't had the natural opportunity to share a bed with Smarm by my own choice and here it was made for me. It was that night, also, that he decided to really push things physically to the next level. Yes, here I am in this totally strange environment with three Labradors on the bed (one his) and people in the next room and . . . no. I am not that kind of girl. So, as soon as his friends left the room and flipped the light switch off, I grabbed onto his dog, spooning him so I wouldn't have to worry about what to do with the guy, and fell asleep.

I thought my plan had worked brilliantly until I woke gradually in the middle of the night to a strange sensation . . . the bed was shaking. What is this? Was Smarmy thrashing in REM sleep? Why did it seem largely directed at me? And, were those his arms clasped around my waist? Seriously?

As I rose out of the fog of dreams into lucidity, I realized what was happening. It requires the use of better descriptors, but I don't write porn: the guy is dry humping me with feeling. It's got to be 2 am. I cannot believe this. Violated does not begin to describe.

I am lying in bed and wondering what exactly I should do about this. Do I pretend I don't notice? What is he thinking? Is this sexsomnia? I am searching for the right thing to do. The stage we're at is just so . . . tenuous I'm not comfortable with any of my choices, so I go for the path of least resistance: I ended up just taking it and eventually he gave up and went back to bed.

Seven A.M. ticked over and the alarm sounded finally, me rising from my prone position (though fully awake all night since the incident) and we set out for the anticipated skiing.

No, I did not mention the nocturnal happenings that disturbed my sleep. For being as outspoken as I am, when it comes to other people, I am foolishly silent sometimes. You'll soon see.

I'm in the back seat when the boys light up (and I don't mean cigarettes), skunky smoke filling the car. Now, I'm not unfamiliar with this particular substance, but one of my biggest pet peeves is people who smoke out when driving - it impairs you just as much as alcohol, I don't care how much of a stoner you are. But hey, I am the new as-the-limit-approaches-girlfriend and I don't want to be a bitch.

I might also note that he's hid his little recreation from me up until this point, so it's also a bit of a surprise.

I lean against the window in the back seat and wiggle my feet. At least I have *lots* of leg room.

When we get on the slopes, I decide to drop the past and live in the moment, thinking, "Wee!"

No, no wee. For these guys, "skiing" apparently means smoking out on the slopes before every run and stopping every second run at the bar to get trashed. Not being of that persuasion, I basically just sat there like a dutiful gal and watched it happen while internally mulling over my complete revulsion for both of them.

A few hours of this go by and we're on the chairlift when the guys start rough-housing and trying to push each other off. At this point I *have* to say something because I have visions of compound fractures of the femur in my future and of course, who's the buzz kill? Yeah, had to be me.

The sun is setting, both boys are wasted out of their minds, so clearly I have to drive home. Yay me. We stop in the foothills at a gas station, and they have the bright idea of getting more beer. As they go inside, I call my buddy in Sac and beg him to save me - but as always, he has a date and can't do it. I might point out that he also never has a girlfriend. I haven't seen him for a few years because every time I want to get together with him, some one-date wonder is occupying his time. This time I'm cursing the stars: the guys are in the car and I can't accurately detail my dilemma so he feels no obligation to save me in any way. The subtlety is lost. Damn you, Dating Buddy, damn you.

They come out with the beer, but I'm thinking, "Well, maybe when we get home and pop these open, I'll drink and it won't be so bad since I'll be on the same page."

Oh, wait, this beer wasn't for going home - it was intended as road beer, as in: beer consumed while in motion in a vehicle. Yes, I am now participating in a felony by driving with open beverages as these fellows get further intoxicated. Fuming, but what am I supposed to do?

I turn the radio up to drown them out. At this point I think they can tell I'm not happy. Just maybe.

I get home, and the boys promptly pass out. The friend's wife suggests she and I pick up burritos for dinner and while we're out she casually comments, "Oh, I should have warned you, they always do this."

Okay, seriously? This is our first trip out, you're dating me and you couldn't at least try to pretend you aren't a total dog?

I mean, she says you *always* do this?

This relationship is over, as far as I'm concerned. Maybe if he'd wooed me along and got me all in love with him and then busted out the bad behavior, I could find a way to live with it the way wifey did - but now? Idiot.

Wifey and I go and get burritos to bring back to the troops and when they rouse, Smarmy's substance-addled brain thinks I totally would love to snuggle with him. I am sitting on the couch next to him, the married couple opposite us, and he's got his arm around me, hand rubbing up on my thigh. I smile like a good Stepford Wife. Can't do anything here without looking like a jerk, so I just take it.

Luckily, we stayed out late skiing so bedtime comes quickly. I am not having any of it, so I grab his sweet chocolate lab and curl up.

2 am. The bed is shaking. Not again.

So, lesson out there, men: you can totally do anything you want, so long as you give a girl her leg room and open doors.

2 FIRST DATE

This is the story about my first official date. You may find it pathetic on a number of levels. The date itself was pathetic, but moreover, the fact that it was my first date and I was eighteen just highlights that I happen to be a huge loser. There, I said it.

I got a job for the summer before college as a Takeout Taxi. Basically, what I did was wear a black polo shirt and drop in and out of mid-range restaurants picking up food and delivering it to people who were too lazy to drive and pick up their own food. These people were also pretty well off because the service was about twenty-five percent higher than getting it themselves, and they still had to tip me.

It was a sweet job on many levels:

I only worked four or five hours a shift and made a hundred or more, easily. Especially when I got to work my hometown area, which is known for an abundance of celebrities who are lose with their Benjamins.

I got to meet Toni Morrison, whose book I had just finished reading. She likes Chinese food and her house had a fancy, emblazoned brass door. I pretended to not know who she was.

I found myself in the kitchen of a famous basketball player who had Bible verses lining the ceiling like molding with "obey" and "honor" in red ominously hanging over dining guest's heads.

I learned all about the short cuts and residential neighborhoods of my county.

I got to talk on a CB radio and had a call sign: KM1.I didn't have to deal with bitchy customers or restaurants as they were kept far away from each other.

I now have, among my many skills, professional knee-driving abilities. It has come in handy more times than I can count. Also great for scaring friends on windy roads: "Trust me, I was a takeout delivery girl. I can do this!"

I was the only girl who did this, and as a result, *all* the guys were into me and not afraid to show it. This was most evident in that the dispatchers would send me the free food pickups and big tip orders. A very big deal, you'll remember, as this is purportedly the story of my first date and I am, I repeat, eighteen.

I had a lot of little flirtations going (which was great for my ego because before then I thought I was a troll): one of the dispatchers absolutely had no limits with me but was engaged and therefore safe, this bigger guy who later admitted he used to show a photo of me to his friends and pretend I was his girlfriend (yes, creepy), some of the cooks (who talked about me in Spanish, but I never let on I understood them), and Sac State Dude.

Sac State Dude was a nice boy, but I didn't really have much interest in him. He was really the only guy who had a chance with me as we were about the same age, same energy level, and not quite as weird as some of the other guys working there. Some of the dispatchers decided we were a match and started telling us so. This led him to start flirting a bit over CB:

"KM1, how's it going?"

"SSD, great! What's your 10-20?"

"KM1, just picking up food at Max's! What you got going on?"

"SSD, just 10-13'd and waiting for a dispatch."

Ahhh, can't you hear it? Love was in the air.

After a few weeks of this, SSD gets the courage to ask me out, and he's clearly nervous about the whole prospect by the wavering in his voice and lack of eye contact as he makes his request when we see each other in person at Tony Roma's: a Place for Ribs.

On one hand, I am really excited: finally someone has decided I'm cute/cool/girlish/alive enough to ask out. On the other, I feel kind of bad for him because I am not as nervous because he just doesn't do it for me.

By that, I should probably point out that those who "did it" for me in high school were people who paid little-to-no attention to me, who I thought were out of my league, and who had nothing in common with me. This would be a clear indication that Sac State Dude was probably The One. The guy I was meant to be with – the absolutely opposite of what I wanted at the time.

The day of the date, I woke up with a bad scratch in my throat which is always my omen of impending sickness. It progressed throughout the day and by the end of my shift, I was full-blown sick. Now, ordinarily someone would have canceled and rescheduled, but he was really into this and remember that this is my first date - ever. What if this was my only shot?

That was strike one.

Strike two was that I had to drive. Sac State Dude was your typical poor college student, which is fairly rare to find in the area I grew up in. Most kids seemed to expect bright cherry-red Mustangs in the driveways on their sixteenth birthdays. SSD had a car, but it was neither bright nor a Mustang, though it was red – and the size of a roller skate. His stereo had broken and he had duct-taped a little boom box to the dashboard to get him through the long hours of our job. It also had a penchant for breaking down, which it did that day.

We met after our shifts ended at eight that night at the local mall and at his suggestion, go west toward Berkeley. It's not a particularly beautiful night in the Bay Area – the fog has rolled in and my windshield wipers are on intermittent. He suggests we drive into the hills, and as I take the sharp corners up, up, up, he asks me about my accent.

I stop short. What accent

He states that clearly I am from somewhere other than California.

"I'm not," I tell him.

"You are," he asserts.

Now, granted, my parents are both from New York. I say "Dad" like "De-ad." And I say, "Route" like "Root" and "roof" is "ruff." But that's about it, I think. I have been chastised at a former workplace for sounding too much like a college Valley Girl – my speech has always been fast, heavily peppered with useless "like"s and its shrill and chirpy. I have the archetypal California blonde accent.

He will not let it drop and decides I am just ashamed of where I come from (which is apparently not the East Bay).

As we career through the fog-encrusted hills, he tells me he's already got a gift for me, but won't tell me what it is: it's for the second date. Uh huh. Already a gift?

It turns out he had designs on ending up at the Lawrence Hall of Science, which is a sweet date place if it's open. I have fond memories of being a very small girl and going there on field trips to find out more about dinosaurs. These dinosaurs *terrified* me as a young girl. I had recurring dreams for ten years that these life-size statues would come get me at my house and chase me through the neighborhood, eventually eating me. I actually had a permutation of this dream all the way through college. I think I've finally gotten over it.

Now, if you happen to be taking me on a date, and you don't know that the place gives me the willies, it's a great choice for first date location. Sitting high up in the hills of Berkeley, it overlooks the bay with a picturesque view of San Francisco's sparkling skyscrapers reflecting in the sea water.

Plus, it's got a badass whale.

No, for serious. A life size, concrete blue whale beached at the entrance circle that you can climb up on and slide around on. On any given day, the popularity of said whale is obvious because no matter how recent his latest paint job, Whaley has butt-rubbing spaces all up and down his spine from people sliding off him. If you see this whale, you cannot resist taking a photo of it doing a silly pose. It is useless to try.

To this day, thoughts of the whale can send me into internal girlish squealing paroxysms, so Sac State Dude made a good call. But, well, you have to remember that I'm fighting a really bad cold. I feel like crap: it's taking all my energy just to maintain conversation and navigate the narrow roads.

I park my car and get out with him and walk out toward the whale. It's dark, foggy, and there are fences all around because of construction.

SSD is downtrodden for a bit before he lights upon a brilliant idea: scale the fences and sit on the whale.

I fold my arms and sniffle, "I dunno, I seriously don't feel so good. I didn't know we'd be out in the elements. I don't have a coat."

He puts his hands on his hips, "Kristin, I asked you out precisely because you're adventurous. How can you say no?"

Oh, there it is, the first time a guy pulls the "adventurous" line on me to challenge me into doing something I don't want to do: including date them.

I come back plaintively with a lot of affected nasal emphasis: "I'm sick?"

He gives me a disappointed, pouty face.

I scale the wall and proudly sit on the whale, sniffling and head swimming.

After the novelty of that wore off, we were back in the car and headed into the touristy area of town far below. His next idea was to go to Blondie's pizza for dinner. Blondie's is a Berkeley icon that delivers excellent, greasy pizza, and it is open late because it is close to the college and college housing.

I wasn't hungry, and I was definitely not up for the standing at the counter aspect of this date (Blonde's is, like many fine establishments in the city, just a window on the street). Nonetheless, I placidly stood there while he enjoyed his greasy wedge.

"What next?" he asked in far too perky a manner.

I chew on my response, finally expelling: "Can I just go home?"

His face fell.

As I drop him off in front of his house, he leans into me and softly asks, "Have you ever kissed anyone in a car?"

No, I admit. I get a little freaked about this . . . am I about to? This is also going to be my first kiss. I have a cold. I am not remotely attracted to Sac State Dude. It's taken all my effort to get to this point. I wanted my first kiss to be a fairy tale . . .

As I'm running this through my head, he finishes his thought: "Well, don't. It's incredibly uncomfortable and stupid. Take my word."

And that's that. He asked me out again, but I said no. No more flirting on the CB.

At least, not with him.

3 IN WHICH I BECOME AN "IT." I THINK.

Being an eternal optimist, I am willing to try pretty much anything someone throws out at me when it comes to finding love. This includes going on dates with people I've never met. While many people avoid blind dates on principle, I figure that friends who set up such things have only the best intentions and probably, if you run the numbers, have better odds of matching you up than most other ways of finding someone can yield.

Of course, it would help if my friends were good at evaluating people's needs.

I frequent the dog park a lot. At the dog park, there's only so much you can talk about and bond over. Everyone's there for the same reason: you have a dog. Though, sometimes there are the freaky lurker people who don't have a dog and just watch everyone. And there are the old ladies who come and set up their folding chairs and gab away planning dinners and gatherings (usually at the dog park) despite not always brining their dog.

I have a few casual dog park friends I make generally because we show up around the same time and at some point, you have to break the ice. It's a lot easier to do this when you have the same breed of dog. I have one such "friend," and I always spend my hour there talking to him primarily because he's close to my age and he's got an older Australian Shepherd that my little Aussie sort of finds interesting.

One day he tells me he has this newly single friend he thinks might be great for me.

Through email, we arranged to meet at one of the summer concerts downtown, and I had pretty much no clue what he looked like but I trusted that my dog park friend wasn't going to do anything mean to me. Dog park friend is pretty cute, and it's my experience that cute people tend to hang around with cute people. I went down with my roommate and some of her friends so that I had an out should something happen.

What would he look like? What would his voice sound like? How would he gesture? How would he dress? It was kind of exciting, since I had no expectations to build upon.

When I met him? Wow. Just wow.

I wanted to throw my hands up and declare victory for dating women on blind dates everywhere. His eyes were dreamy, bedroom blue. His hair was neat and sandy blonde, bleached by days spent riding the waves on the beach. His body reflected good eating habits, athletic pursuits, and probably some rigorous lifting of heavy weights.

This man was far too good looking for me. It was hard for me to even look at him straight.

Dog park friend did a good job - maybe too good of a job. I tend to like guys who are a little less unassuming about the looks. My friend calls it appreciation of the "new hot" and I think that's about right - those of us who at least thought we were geeks in our youth did not grow up "hot" and therefore don't have that air about them.

I have a theory that especially beautiful people have especially boring/unbeautiful essences because there was no adversity to go through - people bend to your every whim. This guy had to be a chump - he was just too pretty.

Anyway, I brought him back to introduce to my roommate and she, too, was like, "Wow."

We enjoyed the concert for a while and then decided to catch a beer down at the nearby pub. I know a couple of the bartenders and after he greets both of us, we realize we knew the same one working there tonight. He offered: "A bit of a slut, isn't he?" I was all about that, because, yeah, I agree, and it was just another common point on which to build.

Of course, when you don't have much to talk about yet, letting the sexual behavior of a mutual acquaintance dominate the conversation isn't a great tactic. At least that's what all the dating books say. Come off as charming and sweet – don't let them see what a vicious gossip you are. As we go to the back patio with our beers, I realize I'm giving him a bad impression of how judgmental I am – I should not have taken the bait. Blast!

As we take a seat outside, I run into a guy I know and engage for a minute or two before turning back to my date. So flustered by the charms of my date, I now realize I totally forgot to introduce him. Strike two! Now I am not only a vicious gossip, but I lack general social charms as well. Yipes!

Truly, this guy is too good for me.

Aside from that, conversation was free and easy and we had enough in common to keep the evening rolling. Most dates end here, but instead we extended into Thai food after the drinks. This guy was good - he ordered for me, which is one of those charming things guys rarely take a chance on. As we close our menus, two professors come up to him and started engaging him in conversation, genuinely interested in what he was up to. They looked at me and told me what a catch I had, assuming we were in a relationship. Lucky, lucky me, I thought. Dog park guy is definitely getting a big gesture of thanks from me. This guy turning out to be the true gentleman I'd been seeking.

The night began to wear down and I found myself on the porch of my house with him. I hate this part of the night – there's an expectation of a first kiss, which I hate, and I never really know what to do. He just stood there. I just stood there.

Finally he offered, "So, I don't know how to do this. I just got out of a six-year relationship and . . ."

Yes! Free! And, me being me, I wanted to diffuse that for him, so I threw my arms around him and said, "I had a good time, and I'd love to see you again. And that's how we do this."

I went inside satisfied with how it ended, but pretty much sure that was the end of that (I have a formula: however long you're with someone, it takes half that time to get over the breakup, and he'd be ready three years from now, if he doesn't get back with her). But one does hold one's hopes up. He seemed like a nice guy, but I wasn't going to sit by the phone waiting for him to call.

A week goes by and nothing, and despite my summation of the evening, I check my phone and email every two minutes or so, just to be sure he hasn't called while I was distracted by breathing or something. By the end, I figure that I was the result of dog park guy going, "You really should think about seeing other girls . . ." and him grudgingly agreeing to it. Or, perhaps I did really blow it with a few of my lesser qualities being aired for all to see. Or, you know, I sure as hell am not a model, it's entirely possible my charms were not for him.

Finally, I get an email time-stamped at 4 a.m. the next Friday. He'd been out of town a week, and wanted to touch base. And what he said was: "I had a good time hanging out with you but I don't think it's what I'm looking for right now."

"It"?

Okay, seriously? What exactly was "it?" Does "it" replace "you?" And what is that really supposed to mean, anyway?

It's not like I contacted him or said at any point in the date what I wanted "it" to be. "It" could have been a freaky-deaky one night stand. It could have been true-love-marriage-forever. What was "it" was for him? Did he spend a week mulling over the date and creating something that wasn't there? Did we have an intense, whirlwind relationship in his head?

And sending it at 4 a.m.? That's quite a story. I wrote back and wished him well, and never heard from him again.

I have to say, though, there is this new trend of dealing with the serious stuff through email that I don't like. Everything is well and good until someone has to do something hard, and then it's typeriffic. I do okay in this medium because I'm an English professor and freelance writer – I'm probably better with text than in person - and I just wonder how normal, non-English teachers/writing mavens manage it.

It's really hard to carry over a serious discussion in email into a real life one. If you can let the sleeping dogs lie and your issues are resolved virtually through the words, it's usually my intention to leave it there and not bring it up in another format. If you start by phone, end by phone. Start in person? End in person. And never bring it up again . . . that might just be a teensy bit dysfunctional or a ton of enlightened.

I have no idea which.

Kristin Tara McNamara

4 DATING AIN'T SAVING THE WHALES

A nice, athletic lawyer-type, the kind my mother would be proud to have in our family, is sitting next to me at the bar. Tonight is special, we have an "in" and the drinks are on the house. So very, very impressive.

I met this guy on a fluke, and the whole reason we were on a date was a bit odd. He challenged me. By this, I mean he literally challenged me to the date. He asked me out randomly (this rarely happens) and when I brushed him off, he indignantly declared that I must be one hell of a loser to not give him, clearly a winner, even one date. He said it with such bravado that I was suddenly very, very confused. In Neil Strauss' *The Game* this would be a very effective "neg." His theory is this: tell the girl who's used to compliments that she's crazy and she'll wonder if that's so and work hard to prove she's not.

So, originally, the date he had proposed was mountain biking up some trail that to this day I do not know exists and then have dinner at the Hof Brau in Shell Beach.

Now, if you are a girl, you are naturally inclined to wonder what the dress code for an evening out is going to be. Shoes can be practical or not. Bra can be cute or not. Hair, up or down? But mountain biking and then casually rolling up to a Hof Brau? *Vogue* does not regularly make recommendations on such occasions.

It drives me crazy, actually. Because, well, when I ride with any seriousness, I have a little get-up - shoes with cleats, bike socks, spandex-chamois pants, spandex shirt, gloves, helmet, right?

But this particular Hof Brau calls for at minimum, some nice pants - not jeans.

And - clearly - not spandex.

I obsess over this for a few hours until I call him and ask him. He negs me again, telling me I am a silly girl for worrying about what I'm supposed to wear. Eventually he concedes that it's a bit of a dramatic first date and instead it's a "let's meet at Mother's Bar for drinks" kind of date during my town's famous evening outdoor Farmer's Market.

I know how to dress for this. Thank the heavens.

As soon as we sit down, he starts up again. Knowing my affinity for my mutt, he asks me about my dog, and as I slowly reveal that I am part of the inner-sanctum of dog-show-people, it turns out we know a few of the same dog people. This naturally leads into talk about how my dog isn't a normal happy-go-lucky Australian Shepherd that he's expecting and that if he were set foot onto my property without an invitation, he'd at the very least be read the riot act by an irate little dog who would not stop at barking.

"Known propensity for biting?" he says. "Hmm, I could easily build a case on that."

He's a lawyer, remember?

Well, he's not just a lawyer. It would appear that he's the type that perk up at the sound of catastrophe, and he just suggested me he could make money off me and my dog.

Help me.

The thing is, I truly believe he can't really mean that, so I persist. The conversation turns to professions, and it turns out he got out of produce distribution (which has huge money potential) to go to law school. I ask him if he likes it and he says, "I rake in the cash, what's not to like?"

I ask him if he feels fulfilled: "We ain't saving the whales here."

At this point, he starts telling me I'm a fool for being a teacher and volunteering my time to help others.

He reminds me again, "In professional life, you shouldn't be out to save the whales."

Actually, you ass, that's precisely the attitude I use when I approach work. As outwardly sarcastic and callous as I can sometimes appear, deep down, all I want to do is save the world and everything on it. And this guy is telling me he could get me a produce brokering job and I could start being a real grown-up. I get this lecture from my mom quite a bit, thank you.

I hate him. I hate him.

My friend comes by randomly and asks me where I've recently moved. She asks for specifics. I don't want him to know but she won't let me evade. I end up giving her precise directions, and as a result I went to bed that night with nightmares of him trying to get himself bitten because I am convinced he really is that evil.

Dinner is done and he suggests we walk around downtown (it's Farmers', and that's what you do here). Unable to extricate myself, I agree.

Suddenly, he shoots out into the crowd and brings back the one person I would really, really never want to meet. There is a guy who has been attending Farmers' since I've been in town that has a hellfire and damnation message on a sign that he walks around with. He has big, late 60's glasses, dyed-black and slicked-back hair, and glossy black OJ Simpson-Isotoner gloves. When trying to communicate the message of his Lord's love, looking like this will get you everywhere.

And . . . this guy wants me to meet him.

While shaking his gloved mitt, I am polite outwardly and inwardly horrified. How these two met, what they have in common . . . it beats me.

As we walk away, he goes for my hand. He's insulted my very core, threatened to take my money through litigation, and he now has me physically in his grasp.

Luckily, the sun is setting and I've ridden my bike to the rendezvous. The strategy was to give myself an out if I wanted, or an in ("Could you drive me and my bike home now that it's dark?"). I tell him I need to go or I will get caught in the dark (not that this bothers me, but he doesn't know that, right?). He stops me in the street, says, "I had a great time: I want to see you again." I smile weakly and nod. He lets go of the grip on my hand and I take off running for the hills.

He never saw me again.

He did, however, teach me that I should not date a guy when his primary mode of engaging me is insulting me. And you may think that's funny, but this seems to be a common tactic people use. At least on me.

5 BABELFISH IS MY BEST FRIEND

"Thank you for calling Lightspeed, a OneMain.com company. How may I provide you with excellent service?"

The year is 2000. I have achieved a dream. A very, very dorky dream: I am a dial-up technical support rep. I worked my way up from the ranks of mere Customer Service Rep to Tech - no pay increase, but far more pride. People often ask why I'm good at computers. I am good, you see, because from age ten to twenty or so, I was a rabid computer geek.

A cute, rabid computer geek, but a geek nonetheless.

I could talk to you about the benefits of a particular component in your computer. My co-workers invited me to LAN parties. Don't know what that is? It's where, before affordable laptops and broadband Internet, people would lug their desktop computers, plug into a network, and play computer games. I had a crush on a guy who played video games all night and whose house was a mess because he couldn't clean. "Doom" was all that mattered. I seriously thought he was pretty cool.

I got a massive kick out of being able to help people solve their problems and teach them the wiles of their scary new computers. DSL was just coming out - just to give you some context here. We all had dial-up. My friends got it free and I was so popular because of that.

And, one of the benefits of being a geeky girl (who also happened to be in a sorority) is that the call center is somewhat devoid of them. All the men liked me. I got some really interesting friends out of the deal, and plenty of weird stories. But I am totally lying to you if I tell you that this is a dating story. It's not: it's a sexual harassment story.

So, call centers are set up so that each of us get our own headset and we sit in cubes with a chat program running and the phone rings through to us - we do our job, enter our reports, and call it good. When something doesn't go right, we go to our lead. The floor usually has two or three leads working it. One of the leads was a pretty cute little blonde chick, but most were just . . . pudgy, angsty tech geeks who'd been at it longer than I.

I say this, because up until the shut the center down, I was in the running for becoming a lead.

And I liked this job so much, I almost quit school for it. I am that geeky. That pathetic.

Anyway, one of my leads, Herr Supervisor, was this tall guy in his forties who wore a gold band, but we all assumed that it was not because he was married. The guy either never did laundry or he never used deodorant because, as nice as I can put it, the guy reeked. It was hard to stay in the same cube as him, much less have him look over your shoulder at your reports.

What I liked about Herr Supervisor, though, was that he had chocolate. Always. Every little break, I'd make a trip to go see the Herr and grab one of the Dove candies he kept. When I made it known how much I liked it, it became a little game for us: I'd see him, and I'd get a chocolate. I would humor his stench in exchange for sweet, sweet confections.

I admit it, I was a chocolate whore.

One day I called in sick to work. Herr Supervisor took it upon himself to send me some links to random sites all day. I found this amount of time spent on me a little weird, but I was polite and thanked him.

The next shift came and it was the same: chocolates + Herr Supervisor.

It wasn't much more time before he started addressing me in German.

Thinking he was a massive freak, I thought nothing about it, but I did tell him that he was being stupid because I didn't speak German, so I hope he was amusing at least himself.

He would just smile.

Herr Supervisor was harmless. Twice my age, no big deal, right?

Until one day he sent me an email.

The email was in German. Now, I have had enough exposure to German to get a general gist of things but I wanted to be sure, so I sent it to my friend who claimed fluency. Like me, he didn't want to jump to conclusions.

I put it through BabelFish (you know, the free Internet translator).

What came up, well . . . it turned out to be a quite raunchy declaration of his love and all the things he wanted to do to me. Things I had not yet done with a svelte, attractive guy my own age, much less stinky ol' chocolate-pimping Herr Supervisor. Things I would have much rather have had done to me by the "Doom" gamer in the dark, filthy one-bedroom apartment.

Horrified and still totally naive, I didn't know what to do, panicked, brought it up to a coworker I trusted, had the guy pulled into the office, suspended, and then taken off my supervision. He slinked around the rest of my tenure there and I did pretty much the same.

And thus it is that Kristin discovers that innocent flirtations and kindnesses can mean a lot more to nerdy men, no matter the age. Also, not to pimp one's kindness in the name of sweets.

6 THE BEST DATE EVER

Have you heard the one about Eskimo words for "snow?" There's thousands! Hundreds! Dozens! This poignant fact is supposed to show us the important cultural significance of language and environment. It's also a bit misleading: when I moved to Mammoth from the sunny and warm side of California, I found out that the English language has zillions of words for the stuff, too: groppel; corn snow; pow pow; sleet; dry; wet; heavy; sticky. You get the idea.

This is the story about how I learned about hoar frost - one of the myriad ways we can describe snow . . .

So I'd just graduated from college and I didn't know what to do with myself and had the good fortune to land a gig in Yosemite National Park up in the high country. Prior to this experience, I imagined the words "alpine" and "high country" to mean completely impassable, monstrous, inaccessible mountains. The world became a lot smaller when I realized that I could get up the peaks of these mountains in less than an hour by walking there from my cabin.

The world is also very small there in a very literal sense. There are probably a hundred people stationed up there for the summer, and unless they are really long termers, they are all twenty to thirty years old. What do twenty-somethings with free-spirit attitudes not pinning them down to an eight-to-five career? That's right, they hook up. With abandon.

I remember my roommate waking up in the middle of the night giggling because she found her ex's beanie cap (that's toque for you Canadians) in her bed and said, "Oh, I busted myself!" How she managed to hook up with him without me being aware of it is pretty good work - we shared a cabin, our beds feet apart. I hope I was away for the weekend, because I know I don't sleep that hard.

Anyway, being both a very good girl and a very picky one, nobody really struck my fancy in Yosemite. Of course, this totally branded me a freak. One of the things you have to understand, though, is that I detest being part of a soap opera plot. My life is pretty straightforward with no regrets because I don't do things people are going to talk about behind my back.

I am sitting in the Visitor Center writing poems about the various hikes in the area to pass the time when my supervisor eyes me a bit and says, "So . . ."

"Yes?"

"I noticed you haven't struck anything up with anyone here."

"Nope."

"Why not?"

"Nobody interesting."

"Mmm hmm."

That's not entirely true. I was harboring a pretty healthy crush on a guy that became a climbing partner of my roommate's. He was goofy, older, and educated and that's really all it takes. He also killed my crush on him when one night we all went out to play pool and I was sizing up my shot when he got right in front of me, unzipped his pants and flashed me his wiener. In public. Nothing says, "Unclassy" like showing off your bits in public for no good reason.

So, one person I happened to know in passing was Southern Janitor Dude. There were two of them, actually. One was really tall and he had white-boy dreads kept up in one of those crocheted hats, and the other was smaller, very pretty on the eyes, and always wore this pink beanie. Pink, like, "I am wearing my girlfriend's hat" pink. I always thought it a bit odd, but he was a nice boy. We didn't talk much though.

As the season wound down, pretty-on-the-eyes Southern Janitor Dude mentioned that he was looking for a place in Mammoth for the winter and I said that I, too, was. That would solve things nicely!

This also precipitated us talking a lot more and I come to find out that he's a dedicated technical mountain climber and has a degree in geology and thinks he'll be doing grad school soon.

Oooh, sparkle!

After a whole summer of, "You do the tax calculations, you went to college" comments, this was a welcome break. I have nothing against people who haven't gone to college, but making me feel weird about it wasn't that fun.

We exchanged numbers and in the end, it didn't really work out because Southern Janitor Dude wanted to go home to North Carolina for a while and I got a different guy to take the room instead. But, I told him to contact me when he got into town upon his return, and hand over a big batch of mix CDs for the road - him trading me a couple electronica albums in exchange.

One day I get a call from him, he's camping in the snow out on the road that goes out to the highway. "Get your butt here," I told him, "where it's warm!" For some reason, he was completely averse to spending some time on my utterly comfortable futon in our spacious and notably warm living room (and it better be - heating places in the rural Sierra costs an arm and a leg) but he would come in to hang out.

Some nights he'd come in and we'd cook dinner together, get a movie, whatever. It was nice because he and I didn't know anyone else in town and we had someone to poke around with. He was really different, a true southern gentleman of a breed one doesn't encounter often in California. To this day, whenever I hear the word "Appalachian" I have to correct people's pronunciation because he was adamant it is "App-a-latch-in," not "App-a-lake-in" according to his soft, hint-of-the-south accent. My roommate and his friends had noticed that we'd grown pretty close and started asking about us, but nothing had developed at this point so I had no idea what to tell them. Just friends, it seemed to me. I am very good at making just guy friends.

One day, after Southern Janitor Dude finally got his own place on the other side of town (which is really maybe four blocks away in a town of 7,000 people), he called me up, asking me to dinner.

Pizza was the plan, but when he greeted me at the door, I was more than confused. Dirtbag Southern Janitor Dude of the Pink Beanie that I'd come to know was gone and standing on my welcome mat was a well-shaven, besweatered yuppie. Khakis, tight little v-neck wool sweater, nice shoes. I, on the other hand, had a beanie, fleece, and down jacket on and shoes with big ol' lugs for navigating the melty snow/ice combination so prevalent around town.

This is when your heroine is not sure whether she has just scored big time (being of the persuasion that finds dirtbag-yuppie conversion ultra hot) or not.

When we get to the pizza joint, Janitor Dude makes an interesting choice: instead of sitting across from me, he sits next to me. I say nothing and treat the evening normally. There are many, many question marks flying over my head at this point, but the pizza is good and it's interesting going.

After pizza, we decide we need to do something, so we decide to try going out to the hot springs in my Impreza. If you have been to Mammoth, you know that out beyond the green church, on dirt roads, you can find a plentitude of hot springs for your soaking pleasure. In the middle of winter, these are pretty impassable. With that said, telling me such things makes me try it anyway, so we bump along the long road at high speeds, plowing the powder out of our way until we finally get ourselves well sunk. Luckily my roommate has given me a shovel (one I carry to this day) to dig out in times of trouble, and this is what we do.

Now, remember, Kristin has a down jacket. Southern Janitor Dude, only a sweater. We take turns with the jacket: one digging, on standing and warming. We're successful and still I continue to plow forward. On the fourth got-stuck-and-dig, despite my really enjoying the primal need to act on our survival and the adventurous nature of things, we decide to give up driving and try walking.

The night is dark, it's crisp, and our breath hovers like spirits above our heads as we crunch through the moonlight. We pause for costume changes frequently, trading my down jacket. One such pause, I hear this distinct cracking and cock my head.

"What is that?"

He smiles at me, "Whorefrost."

"What?"

"Whorefrost."

"Say it more slowly."

"Whore. Frost."

"Whore, like hookers?"

"No, like . . . "

"Spell it."

"H - O - A - R."

"HOAR frost? You're making that up."

"Am not. That sound is it developing, growing from the dew in the air and cracking." With that, he goes over and kicks at the embankment of snow surrounding us. Little crystals skitter across the surface, sounding like broken bits of plastic, scraping the frozen surface of the snow. I'm fascinated as they sparkle like a special effect and reach down to feel the sharp shapes, tossing them on the snow and listening to them crickle and sparkle.

The moon is high, he's standing close, the country is beautiful - bathed in a cool bluish hue, and the hoar frost is growing and snapping in the silence. It is one of my life's most perfect moments.

But Southern Janitor Dude stops it, shivering in my jacket: "Can we go home? I am freezing." I snap back to reality, "Oh, yeah, okay."

Nothing happened that night.

After that, Sweater Dude completely disappeared, along with Dirtbag Dude. No more phone calls, no more pizza, nothing. He didn't return my phone calls to invite him to blues shows or fondue parties. My friends asked me where he was, and it smarted to tell them I had no idea.

What happened that night? For a long time I would drive around town, craning my neck for him around every corner, wondering what had happened. Never caught a glimpse.

I did run into him again, though: almost literally.

I was in Yosemite's Camp 4 (the traditional campground base for climbers), hurriedly breaking down my and my partner's tent and stuffing it into my car. My partner's gear had pulled on a climb and where gear and rope usually is there to save you when you fall, it popped out in a ghastly zipper motion and he cratered on the rocks below, bleeding and flopping like a fish. At that moment he was on a helicopter to a hospital in Sacramento and I was trying to hurry to meet him there after collecting our things (by the way, he turned out to be remarkably fine).

As I am getting into my car, I look up to find Southern Janitor Dude standing over me with the CDs I'd lent him six months before. He saw me in the campground and said he'd felt guilty for hanging on to them for so long. We hugged, but I was near tears over what had happened to my partner, offered a short explanation, and drove in a fog to Sacramento. We were both disappointed we couldn't catch up.

It's good to know he didn't die, or something.

I don't know what the lesson is to this one: how the best date of my life to this day (was it a date?) could lead to the death of a well-established friendship is beyond me. Was it something I did? Some inner demon of his? Don't know, but this is one of many in a long line of ambiguous interactions with men.

It seems to be a gift of mine.

7 ENTHUSIASM IS NOT ALWAYS A GOOD THING

So, I have a fiancé in Canada. Not many people know this. My true soul mate, we've done umpteen road trips, never fought, have similar trials and tribulations, like the same music, read the same books, and grow together from afar. I love her.

Yup, I said "her."

Ellie is a girl friend of mine from high school. We've always gotten along really great and at the conclusion of one road trip, we got engaged. Somewhat forced upon her as she was hiding out in California under the radar of the government working at a horse training facility and realized she couldn't go on doing that, she had to move back to her native land as she was technically an illegal alien. On break from grad school, I helped pack up her stuff - along with two rabid kitties - and we drove north in a big U-Haul through California, Oregon, Washington, and British Columbia to arrive in Kelowna at her parent's house.

I spent the days leading up to Christmas with her family and we talked about how she would get back to California one day.

We went skiing, took in things like Canadian liquor stores (which are pretty fun if you're just visiting - the giant beer cooler, the conveyor belts . . .), pickle-flavored popcorn, Tim Horton's, trying to go curling, and arranging flowers. One night, our hot, nearly nude bodies boiling in her parents' hot tub, I couldn't take it any longer: I pledged to her that when they legalized marriage in California, I would marry her. Neither one of us figured any guy we met would mind: "Oh, don't mind her, she's just my wife. We married for convenience." She agreed, and thus I now have a fiancé.

We joyously told her parents, who completely flipped out, being very conservative Canadians. They totally think I am a red, commie influence on poor Ellie.

Anyway, they legalized marriage here in California, but I'm still single. To tell you the truth, I feel slighted. I pledged my love to her years ago and it stands for nothing.

Of course, prior to that, we'd talked about how well we got along and why we couldn't just be happy with each other. "But you just don't do it for me, Kristin," she told me once, via email. Being persistent, I've always looked past those warnings.

Anyway, I kid, I kid. Ellie and I love each other and I would totally marry her if it meant bringing her back, but we both like dudes. This is also why we tend to trade war stories. She doesn't really date as much as I do, so she has more of "crush" stories, and I've tried to hook her up from afar with no luck. Sometimes we surf Match.com for each other and rate the guys.

Ellie, I might add, lives in Calgary and has a far deeper pool from which to skim.

Anyway, Match.com had a free month trial going so we decided we'd sign up and give it a try. I diligently filled out my profile and posted it, afraid someone I knew would see.

No real interesting bites that month, so I canceled my subscription and chalked it up to experience.

Except, a day later, I had an email in my inbox.

It would seem that a guy had seen my profile and marked it to contact me later, but I pulled it by then. I'd left enough bread crumbs about who I was, that he was able to figure out I ran the town's climbing gym and then Google stalk me once he figured out my name (and I am eminently Google-stalkable).

He wrote me a really engaging email and told me that since I'd disappeared, the first thought he had was that my profile was a dummy one that they used to get guys to spend their money. He came off as intelligent, articulate, and we had quite a bit in common from what he told me. Plus, come on, the guy thought I was so cool, he did research to find me. None of this passive crap, he cut right to the chase and made a huge gesture of courtship which any girl can appreciate. I was totally flattered.

We met for dinner after I saw we had good phone chemistry, and it's my usual gesture to pay for my own meal just to make it clear my expectations in dating are to be even-steven. Sadly, I'd left my wallet behind and I apologetically had to take his gift of food. I soon got over that as he continued to impress me with his ambition and animation. He was balls out about what he wanted - career, fun, and me. I have grown to appreciate that immensely in a man.

Dinner was good, I looked awesome, and things were great until dessert arrived. I posed a question naively to him when I saw there was a maraschino cherry perched atop our tempura ice cream, "So, can you tie the cherry stem with your tongue?"

His eyes glinted and he waggled his head a bit, "Oh yes, I am *very* good with my tongue."

I could not stop my eyes from rolling - Lord knows I tried. Yeah, okay, I set it up, he knocked it down (albeit via cliché'), and he was so forward that it was kind of hot.

We went out again, only this time on a hike. I always have a bit of a complex about hiking - it's a good way to gauge fitness against other people. Who's sweaty? Who's winded? It's usually me. That's why I hate it. This time, I really wasn't worried.

On the way down from the mountain, he asked me what seemed like a natural question: "So what's your heritage?"

I popped off a casual, "Lithuanian, Polish Jew, and Irish."

He looks at me sideways, as I pick my way down the steep, gravelly descent, "How'd you like a little more Irish in you?"

I look up at him in confusion, lose my footing, and end up sliding a bit on my butt. "What?"

"Get it?"

The wheels are turning. The gears are grinding the rust away . . . old jokes, old joke, what is he imp------- OHHHHHHHHHHHHHHHHHHHHHHHHH.

He. Did. Not.

Oh yeah, he did.

Sometimes you just wish a guy could shut his trap. He was doing so well.

But, I persisted. He was exciting; he was interesting; he was pursuing the heck out of me. We'd meet at the downtown coffee shop, me grading, him doing engineering homework. It was comfortable: it was nice.

And at the end of every little date, he'd send me home smacking my head, trying to get out the echoes of some really stupid sexual cliché'.

You see, there truly is an art to seduction. They have enormous sections of every big bookstore devoted to it. I've read them, even though they're meant for guys. And in big, red print, they tell guys not to act like idiots. Girls are seduced by subtlety. This guy might as well have just pulled out his penis and pointed at it and grinned. The chase was really growing uninteresting, but I really wanted to look past it.

One day, we're doing our coffee shop thing and he asks me when I'm going to do a ride-along with him. You see, this particular guy is rabid about sky-diving. He does a lot of other things, but dropping through the sky is his big fix in life. He really wants me to do it. I have unequivocally told him this will not happen unless it comes free: I can think of a lot of things I can do with a couple hundred bucks that I'd like more than paying to jump out of a plane.

The ride-along is basically "this is my girlfriend supporting my hobby" behavior. You see, I would see him suit up in his little jumpsuit, I would sit with him in the loud, old jalopy as it took off, and I would marvel at his skills and bravery as he jumped from it like a professional. This, according to the seduction books (and more importantly, one my favorite movies, *The Tao of Steve*) is a guy demonstrating his value.

But, see, I'm not that kind of girl. For one, I am not so into this guy that I want to give up my afternoon to "support" him as he jumps from his plane. Two, I don't like "being the girlfriend" in that I sit on the sidelines and wait for him when he's done. I do stuff too, or I let you do your stuff in peace. Maybe down the road, when I am invested, I will want to do it because I love you, but I don't beg you to go to dog shows, don't make me watch you jump out of a plane.

This was, however, a pretty strong indication to me that we were entering the "put-up or shut-up" phase of the relationship, so my radar was on - is this someone I really want to commit to? Do I want to be watching him jump out of planes in the future?

This guy clearly wants to make me his girlfriend. There's no doubt in my mind. I want him to be someone I want to commit to, but there's something holding me back . . . I can't my finger on it . . .

Oh yeah, the bad sexual clichés.

One night, I call him to see what's up and set up another get-together, and he goes, "Hang on a minute."

Insert muffled talking here. Insert laughter. He comes back on the line, "Did you hear that?"

"No?"

"Well, I was talking to you, and my roommate came home and asked what I was doing. I told him I was talking to you, so he said, 'So that's why your pants are down and the anal lube's out?' And I am all, 'No, that's just multitasking! I was waiting for you! Let me put her on hold!' Ha ha ha ha! Isn't that funny?"

No. No, not really.

Lesson learned: sometimes balls-out confidence is just balls-out immaturity. And this guy had to keep his balls in for just that very reason.

8 ALL DRESSED UP AND UP TO GO

I am the one-date queen. For the longest time I thought something was wrong with me: if *I* wanted it to go beyond one date, it wouldn't. If *he* did, I was definitely not on board. Afraid of commitment? No, not really - there are just a lot of frogs to kiss and I tend to have enough sense not to have long make-out sessions with slimy frog lips when the prince does not appear.

One kiss, or nothing. Sometimes the frog grows a little hair or his eyes look just a little more human after the kiss, and I'll keep him around, but so far it's just a mirage and the frog's just a frog.

Wow, I'm a chick kissing a whole pond o' frogs. I'm not sure that's how it's supposed to go. The princess in the story only kisses one. In the real version of the story, the princess smashes the little guy's brains out in disgust. So, I wonder if I am going to be that watered-down version that we all know, or the Grimm Brother's version and end up in the national news for beating my prince to death when I find him?

With that said, who wants to go on a date? Anyone? A show of hands?

Anyway, that one month I was convinced to sign up for a Match.com free trial, I found that I had a few frog prince

candidates to give it a whirl with. I went on a couple of dates .
with no sparks, but one really stands out.

This guy really didn't stand out from anyone, but I went
out with him because he was athletic, outdoorsy, and I
figured it would be a good time. He told me he was attracted
to me because I purported to be athletic, and there are so
very few girls who truly are that.

When he asked me out, he told me the time and day,
but not what we'd be doing. Girls hate that. Why? Because
while guys can wear whatever and look fine and be
comfortable, girls cannot. I am not a girly girl, but I like to
look cool on first dates - sometimes that's a skirt, sometimes
it's nice jeans, whatever. You can usually tell if I'm not
holding out much hope for you if I forgo the eyeliner and
am wearing a t- or polo shirt: I am not trying.

So when this guy arrives at my door, he tells me we're
going hiking! Cool, I think, looking at my t-shirt and jeans
ensemble. I have some flat, kind of nice shoes on, but
nothing in town is unscalable in this outfit.

Or so I believe.

He asks me if I've ever done the "Tower Trail." The
what? I've lived in this town for years and I have been all
over by now, but no, I had not. The Tower Trail was his
intended destination.

If you do not know about Tower Trail, let me be the
first to tell you that this is a trail that's not to be hiked in cute
little flats and tight jeans. This is a trail you hike up in order
to train your heart to sustain you on snowy, alpine ascents.
This is a trail you bring a bottle of water on, sunglasses, and
a sweat band.

This is a trail that goes up. It doesn't meander through
beautiful forests: its sole purpose is getting you to the top the
fastest way possible.

Me: "Huff huff, so . . ."

Him: Not having it. Also, not huffing.

I might also take this time to add that thanks to
incredibly loose joints, I've dislocated my knees about fifteen

times each and unless the stars are aligned properly in terms of supplements, hydration, and weight training, hiking uphill can really hurt. I don't have much cartilage left in there, so each impact crunches down and grinds into the head of my bones - my patella scraping uncertainly along.

I also try not to bitch too much about it until I know you. If I am on a first date, I do not know you well enough to complain.

Me: "You are really going . . . fast."

Him: "Oh, sorry. Anyway, so I mountain bike this trail."

Me: "Huff, huff, hey, can we stop and look at the view?" (Subtle; very, very subtle.) You bike up this?"

Him: "Well, no, there's a different approach."

Me: (desperately trying to catch my breath and start a conversation) "People can ride this trail? You can? That's crazy."

Him: Silent, and clearly not a conversationalist.

So, there I am, hiking painfully, my heart ready to explode out of my chest and trying to make the best of this date - my cute little flats welling up with sweat, since these are not shoes you wear socks with, and causing blisters.

We finally make it to the top, and the view is spectacular. I feel a huge sense of accomplishment, but the biggest reward is the big orange lookout tower waiting. Don't care how bad my knees hurt, towers must be climbed.

And, when one climbs towers in tight jeans that are slightly damp from intense hiking effort, jeans are a little compromised, it turns out. I flipped my leg over the first strut only to hear a "riiiiiiiiiiiiiiiiiip."

I look down. The area that usually covers my inner thighs is no longer there - soft, pale flesh is spilling out attractively. It is only going to get worse from there. These, I might add, are designer jeans - very, very expensive, and very, very non-durable.

I am sitting on the top of this tower with this guy, trying to hide my newly created ventilation holes and I'm looking at him: no chance this is happening. He really doesn't seem all that interested in making this even a little less uncomfortable.

And suddenly, I get it - this guy put me on this trail, knowing full well I wasn't dressed appropriately, to see if I could hang. In a way, this is ingenious if "athletic girl that can keep up with you" is a deal breaker, but I am far from lying about my fitness. Putting me in tight jeans and non-functional shoes and pushing me up the steepest hill in town is not going to make me shine, exactly. This wasn't a date; it was a fit-test.

I ruined my jeans and feet for this?

9 MOTHER KNOWS BEST

My mom really doesn't ask too much when it comes to guys I am seeing. They should have the following qualities for her approval: Catholic, Lithuanian or Polish, and Catholic. That's about it; though I am pretty sure "white" is an unspoken requirement, also. I had not really managed to bring one home that fit those loose requirements until I met Charles.

Now, there is something very sinister in me when it concerns my mom. She's very much a parrot-thinker. She retains a lot of information but doesn't apply it, if that makes sense. What she sees on Fox News is gospel truth. Her life is absolutes. When I left the Catholic Church, she earnestly asked me what was going to keep me from murdering someone . . . uh, basic human values? For this reason, I like to torture her, just a teeny bit. When I lived completely platonically in a tent with a guy for three months in Yosemite Valley, I let her think her worst, "You're not having SEX with this boy, are you? You don't want to be a tramp! You've barely known him!"

"Maybe I *want* to be a tramp? Did that ever occur to you?"

When she mentions drug use, I like to drop hints about things I may or may not have done, just to keep her guessing. I like to make use of my wide knowledge of taboo things just to zing her a little. To this day, she's adamant my brother never, ever masturbated. But she's not entirely innocent, which is why I can play this game: it works.

Now, for a slightly antagonistic relationship at best, we're pretty close. I pretty much tell her everything that won't annoy me later (because she remembers *everything*), but I usually keep away from the guy comments unless I think they are going to stick for more than a few visits. I also do my best to stroke her periodically when it occurs to me that she's set up good parenting moments that, at 28 years of age, I'm now thankful for. I will call her immediately upon one of these flashes and she will really appreciate it, and then make some comments about how unappreciated she feels.

What can I say? We have a very "special" relationship. It's kind of fun now that I get how she works.

So, when I met Mr. Perfect, I called her up and told her I had a dream date lined up: he was both Catholic and Polish. And as a bonus, he hailed from the East Coast (where my parents are from). Oh, Mom was so excited, and she needed to know every single detail about him for the short time that I knew him.

Now, Mr. Perfect has the very clear distinction of actually dating me the "right" way throughout the courtship - by which I mean taking me out to a fancy restaurant, ordering wine, driving, etc. I'm a bit old-fashioned and I appreciate being on that level: Lord knows I don't expect princess treatment, but it is a very gentlemanly way to behave.

Anyway, Mr. Perfect was a pretty attractive dude - tall, dark, handsome, well-built. He looked really great sitting across from me at fancy restaurants and cruising around in his wheels. I was proud to have him as my arm candy. He thought the same thing about me. We had enormous chemistry.

He was recently back from a discharge from the military after having served as a logistics/engineer guy in Iraq. Now, if you know me, that should raise a few red flags. One, most people in the military are fairly conservative, and I am way more left of that. Two, military guys do not get my heart a-flutter. Too meticulous in the ways they go about doing things - I am an appreciator of spontaneous activity and stupid adventure.

Also, Mr. Perfect drove a Bimmer. Now, I have nothing against BMWs. Or luxury cars. Except, you have to understand, that I was raised not to value expensive things for the sake of expensive things. He said he bought the car because when he was in Iraq, that was what he had promised himself he would do when he got home. I thought it was very materialistic of him, and the BMW was suped up and perfectly manicured. Again, nothing against that, but I have something of a fantasy about the cars guys drive that started in college. I like guys who have modest wheels: they aren't pretentious, they are practical, and it shows that they haven't yet "maxed out" in their potential - they are still on their way. That's something I find very attractive. Maybe it won't be so pretty when I'm fifty.

Mr. Perfect had a real passion in life. He was a Parrothead.

What is a Parrothead? A rabid Jimmy Buffett fan. This is another notch on my "mother would approve" belt. It was a bit of an odd hobby. He looked for *every* opportunity to bring it up in the course of a conversation, with me, with my friends, whatever. Nothing wrong with a passion, but this is one I just could not get behind, nor understand. Most Parrotheads are in their fifties. Normally people's affinities intrigue me? This one definitely didn't. It just reminded me of old, lazy people on the beach.

The "buts" kept piling up . . . totally different ideas about what we wanted out of life, out of a home, out of a family . . . it was really hard to find common ground except that we both were totally drawn to each other for inexplicable reasons.

The final straw for me was one night where Mr. Perfect was trying particularly hard to impress - and we went to a restaurant on the water and he ordered some wine. He picked a dry Riesling, which is pretty light, but sweet white vino. When it came to the table, it was insanely sweet - like mead, if you've ever had that. Poor Mr. Perfect was squirming for some reason, but by now he should have figured out that a crummy wine choice wasn't going to destroy my opinion of him. Heck, I like sweet stuff. A lot.

We started talking about religion, and how I'd left it behind. He couldn't believe it: how could I not believe? I told him basically that once I'd found some holes, I couldn't go on pretending just for the sake of what was comfortable or safe. I said, "I mean, look at the Old Testament - I can't believe that Adam and Eve is anything but a creation myth. Not with everything I know."

Mr. Perfect leaned back, smiling, "Oh, but I discount that book. That's silly. Of course all that stuff's nuts and unbelievable."

"But, Charles, the Old Testament is part of your faith!"

"Nah, the New Testament is the real stuff.

"And you think nothing in there is farfetched?"

"What, like the ark? Two by two? Pshaw."

"Okay, so . . . water into wine. Raising the dead. Walking on water. Loaves and fishes."

" . . ."

Poor Mr. Perfect. I had resoundingly shut his heretical logic down. And in that same moment, I realized I couldn't respect a man that held so many untested beliefs that I didn't agree with. When he went to put his hand on my thigh that night on the drive home, I felt nothing.

We both got on instant messenger that night and enjoyed a good chat, but eventually I had to tell him I couldn't go on this way. We didn't have a thing in common.

Mr. Perfect wouldn't have it. He upped his flirting ante. I ate it up. My mind and my heart (and my lust?) were pulling in different directions. I wanted to keep up our banter, our thing, but I knew that in the long run, it would only lead to mutual heartbreak or I'd break down and lose what was important to me (being a bit of an over-giver), so I had to cut ties.

Kind of a bummer, but you gotta know when to hold 'em, and know when to fold 'em. Mr. Perfect needed a girl who wanted a guy like him: he had set himself up to be the quintessential successful guy; whose goals were owning a large tract-home, having big-screen TVs, and a big, Catholic family with whom he'd watch Monday night football. That just wasn't me.

But, tell that to my mom. If he had been a dentist, she would have driven down here and forced marriage on the spot.

10 YOU AND YOUR OPINIONS

So, the other day, a friend who is engaged asked me what a single person does to meet people in a tiny, isolated town like San Luis Obispo. My eyes rolled up and I thought about it: seeing as how I don't work with people my own age, nor in a service industry, and I am kind of set in my social/extra curricular circle - it's actually really hard for me. There's the climbing gym I run, but that doesn't really work since I don't go much and I think it may be kind of weird for guys since I run the place and I'm one of, like, three girls there; the occasional try at Internet dating - but I kind of think that nets a lot of people who have some issues, so I've given that up; random encounters; and, the dog park.

Ahh, the dog park. I've actually scored quite a few guys here. I don't really have the kind of dog that I can take into the public and use as a dude magnet. The Fury pretty much believes all strangers can go straight to hell, so I might force her occasionally to take a pat and she definitely looks like she resents it. But the dog park is different: Fury is a rock star at the dog park.

See, I don't just have a dog. I have an Australian Shepherd. And I have a working-line Australian Shepherd -- fully trained. She can run circles clockwise or counter-clockwise on my command, she can turn left and right, get out, come in, heel, catch Frisbees with back flips, etc. She dunks herself in the little buckets of water and everyone just laughs and laughs. She has been the subject of many a stranger taking a cell phone photo to share with friends.

"Did you see that?"

"Yeah, she always does that."

"Oh. Hee hee!"

Anyway, the Fury is a dog-park rock star. It gives me the in with dudes, especially athletic dudes, who appreciate a dog with some hustle to her. She's feisty.

The usual in is something about "What kind of dog is that?" and before I know it, we're talking. Now, lest you think I am a dog park slut - I keep to myself there. There are all these old ladies that show up from 4:30-5:30 with lawn chairs - I used to be a part of that crowd, too, with my old dog: complete with folding chair. Now I am a free agent. I see a couple people who are regulars and we chat and hang out, but mostly, it's me and the Fury and both of us think strangers can go to hell.

So, this guy comes up to me and somehow gets the *in* with us: Fury decides he's good people and drops the ball at his feet, running around him like she's sling-shotting off him.

He talks really, really fast. Like, okay. I talk fast. I had a couple profs who told me so and made it their job to drive me nuts about this - and when you make me nervous, I talk faster. I gave a eulogy for one of my mentors at a memorial service and after, people told me to slow down. I'm talking to 200 people! I am allowed to talk fast and be nervous! But this guy? This guy talks fast.

And he talks fast because he's got an agenda he wants to share with me.

"You know why people get sick? Dis-ease? Everyone always treating the symptoms but never the cause . . ."

On and on. And the funny bit is, I already completely agree with him. But he's one of those types: the types that argues for the sake of argument. And because of that, when I find a weak spot, I dive in.

My hackles are up. My spider sense is tingling. Weakness in logic! I am so there. I am Going. To. Shut. Him. Down.

I don't know what is wrong with me. I think I would have made an excellent lawyer; I really get worked up when I sense flawed logic. It's like the ultimate challenge. I rise. It's one reason why I love in-person meetings that involve conflicts. I like watching it, and I like participating.

And I mirror people's behavior . . . so I start talking really fast, too.

That lasts for an hour.

I get home and I tell my roommate about this guy who frustrated the heck out of me at the dog park. She looks at me with a sparkle in her eye. "You *like* him, don't you?"

"I don't think so. He's just totally infuriating!"

"Nah, you like that. Those passive guys you've been bringing around - you need a challenge."

Maybe. But I didn't see him again and completely forget all about it.

Fast forward a few months. I'm in an utterly complicated relationship with a guy a couple hours away. We hit it off really well and then he got a job elsewhere. We decided we had to give it a go. But we also didn't really want to make it too serious because . . . "Dude, I have a sweet life, do I want to move? I don't even know what I want from this." And he is thinking, "Dude, I just got to a new place. This is too new a relationship." That's simplifying it, but you get it. We weren't fully committed to anything, really, but we were at the same time. Wee, that's fun. I'll never do that again.

Anyway, so I'm in the middle of that when this guy shows up again on his mountain bike. Now, I don't only have the draw of the Fury, but I'm a few weeks out of surgery and I have a sling on. The sling is also a great conversation starter.

He's charming this time, and he talks just as fast and excited. The hackles go up - I find him electrifying. I want to spar with him. He asks me, "You ever play speed Scrabble?"

"What's that?"

"Come over, and find out."

"Maybe . . ."

I mention how I'm worried I'm going to get all fat without biking everywhere - since I think I'm going to be in the sling for a long time.

"Oh, I'll lend you my trainer!" See, that's a sign, right there. Implied long term loans. The guy is interested. His hackles are up, too. He wants to tango, too.

But here I am, wondering whether I should even be playing along or not. I decide it isn't a big deal, so when I leave, and he asks for my number, I give him it. Guys never call when they ask for the number, anyway. Get cold feet, just want the ego boost, whatever.

Not an hour later, I get a text: "Your assignment: Write one paragraph about the last time you gave your number to a stranger. Email me." He provides his email.

A challenge! I am highly intrigued. It's a really good tactic. I smile, shake my head, and . . . do it. What's the harm?

Then, I call up a friend we both know (because the town is so small, you inevitably trade who you know so you can figure out what circles you run in) and when I ask after the dog park guy, he tells me that this guy is . . . intense. Really? You think? He lets me make my decision for myself.

A reply comes back - right away: no games here, and it's very flirty. I take some time to digest it.

He says he approves of my English skills. The text was a way of screening me. He says he can't stand bad spellers. There are at least four misspellings in his email.

Before I even have time to reply, he sends another email, a little poke. Intense. This guy knows what he wants. That's refreshing. It is also a bit of a warning flag.

He asks if I laughed at his email, and wonders how much Ani Defranco I own.

Okay, what? Ani Defranco is actually a pretty good folksy musician. But generally? I think she's best for pretentious MFA students who sit around with black berets and cigarette holders at coffee house poetry slams. I was introduced to her by the theatre crowd in college. They are one step up from my coffee house MFA student vision, but it's a very short step. I say as much.

He comes back at me with his dukes out. Wanna fight? Ani Defranco is the best musician on this planet! And who am I to critique his English? (I dunno. Who is he to judge people while erring himself - and actually, I'm quite qualified to, if I feel the need.)

He comes back again . . . and I am so incensed, so . . . gosh, I want to strangle him. I have a feeling physical intimacy with this man would be SO fun.

But . . .

Guilt settles in . . . what do I do? Should I tell the guy I'm seeing? But . . . we aren't committed like that, right? But . . . we are, sorta. Ugh. Don't know what to do. Decide to email him back, and tell him basically that I'm in a relationship with someone and I don't know what it is, exactly, so, thanks for playing, but I don't think I should take it any further.

He emails back - "This is all lost on me. You seem like a cool gal but you don't seem interested in simply getting to know people you might click with, which is a bit strange to me. Once you finally tell me where you stand, I'll be listening."

Oooooh, it's a challenge. I want to meet it. "You are cool, but you're being lame." I am not lame.

I will . . .

my fingers hover over the keyboard . . .

I take them off.

I move the mouse.

I hit "archive" (it's Gmail, never delete!).

I will not respond.

You see, I've learned. I've been on too many dates with people that *challenged* me, *incited* me, and I have always mistaken that for confidence and allure - now I tend to think it is more like someone making up for some serious messed-up-in-the-headdedness. I don't need a guy to fight with, thankyouverymuch. I have a nice guy far away that is already screwing with my head. But at least he doesn't want to make me fight him.

Months go by and he texts me another challenge: "I saw you the other day downtown. Decide to make the right decision?"

Exasperated, I look at this text. It's 9 pm on a Friday night. I'm out with friends. Hackles are up.

I don't need this kind of drama.

The right decision is "delete."

11 I REALLY LIKE YOU, BUT REMIND ME YOU EXIST

I have always really liked engineer types. It must be an "opposites attract" thing: I love how meticulous they can be (yet how creative), they come with very unusual hobbies (in college, this included creating fireworks), and lots of them have glasses. I am a sucker for glasses.

So much so, that in Junior high, I used to wear this girl's glasses while I did my science homework. I earnestly hoped it would mess up my eyes, and then I, too, would need glasses. The plan didn't work. I still have phenomenal vision.

And even though I think glasses are cute, I've grown to appreciate opening my eyes in the morning and seeing stuff. So all those of you out there, don't worry, I know I've got it good.

The funny part, though, is that when I tell this story, people inevitably suggest I just get glasses without any correction if I like it so much. These people always seem earnest. But, come on, I *know* that if I showed up one day with glasses, that very same suggester would think, "Man, what a TOOL!"

Anyway, so I thought I really scored big time when a new aeronautics professor asked me to dinner during my grad school days. Nerdy? Check. Good looking? Check. Enginerd? Check. Glasses? Oh, definite check.

While dinner was fun, nothing happened. But, considering my past of finding out that if you let things come on slowly, sometimes you're blindsided, I'm always one to play things out and not worry about it. Chemistry is a wonderful thing, but slow-burn friendship works, too (except when it results in unrequited love, so one must be careful there).

I do think that I'd be remiss if I didn't make a comment about this, as this has long been a problem for me. One - I am the quintessential "guy's gal" - I get that. I'm fairly "tough" physically, and most of my friends are guys. I probably don't give off the cute, sweet "girl" vibe most guys are looking for when dating because I don't have much conditioning that way. This is me owning my problems, in case you haven't noticed.

But with that said, I seem to get trapped into these limbo-esque situations where I don't know what the guy wants - and that makes me utterly crazy. Once I figured this out, I decided it was just safer to assume they didn't want anything, but it's still pretty weird. I think we're in a strange social period of life: we're all well socialized for professional life, but no one teaches us how to "date." Except, perhaps, Neil Strauss and Dr. Phil.

Is this compounded by the fact that I'm totally turned off by the aggressive, meathead guys that hit on me in bars and I'd rather have the shy guy? Probably. But damn, people, go after what you want. If you don't, you'll get what you've always got. And if you're rejected? Well, then today is just like yesterday, and yesterday was not so bad, was it?

So we kept going out. He would drop me off in front of my house, but never make a single move, and seemed fairly averse to coming inside. Now, not like I am the clichéd urban-hip chick who invites you inside for a "nightcap" and doesn't mean a drink - but generally I am very curious about people's living situations, especially when I am dating them. You can tell a lot about a person by their house, right?

Anyway . . . so the quarter started to wrap up and we were both really busy (me with papers and grading and him with grading and research), so he sent me an email to the effect of:

"I am having a wonderful time with you, but life is really busy and I need to focus on work. If I forget to call you at the beginning of the quarter, please give me a poke.

Whaaaaaaaaaaaaaaaaaaaaaaaaaat?

You're kidding, right? "I think you're awesome, but I may forget you exist, so remind me." Yeah, no.

I couldn't even be polite; I was so mad. No matter how you look at it, that's not good. It's not even nice.

I wrote him back in response to his cowardly email and told him that there was no point in pursuing something if he thought he might "forget" about it.

Wow.
Serious, serious "ouch."

Kristin Tara McNamara

12 LOVE IS A ONE-SIDED PRISON

Back in college the theatre crowd would get together for fun times consisting of poker (wherein they'd take my money but ply me with wine) or lights-off tag. I love that the theatre people weren't too cool to party with games like that. There'd be twenty, thirty, of us all milling around in this dark house trying to avoid the seeker. I can't remember what the ultimate goal was, but it was fun.

Anyway, I feel like the search for healthy love is like the tag-in-the-dark game.

In trying to avoid getting hurt, most of us have the bad fortune of stumbling around in the dark and just grabbing on to the first thing we bump into to keep us upright. Others run into someone with a flashlight, or at least a good idea of the layout of the land who's willing to share. Some of us just keep bouncing off the surfaces we encounter hoping to stay in the game until someone finds the light switch and the party resumes, and I happen to be one of those.

When I was younger, though, I was a bit prone to following people around hoping they were concealing a flashlight and were just waiting for the right time to share. Sure, they might shrug me off, but I am tenacious. When I got it into my head that I liked someone, I'd latch on and do everything I could to make them see what a catch I was. Funny how that never worked for me. Wasted a lot of time and emotions on it, too.

I recently had a slightly awkward conversation involving most of my friends and a guy I briefly spent a little dating time with but ultimately decided to call it. He was lamenting that no girls seemed to like him and he was probably just someone meant to be alone forever. Always wanting to dive into that, it was sort of hard - considering that I happened to be one of the girls he was complaining about, but we entered into the conversation about how girls can get run down by a persistent guy, but it never works in the reverse.

Guys like the chase, I guess.

Anyway, most of my undergraduate career was spent pining over someone that really, really didn't want me. He liked me fine, and we got on well. Spent a lot of time together, but he was just not having it. He would give me just enough to hold out hope, but never enough to justify it. I still wish my friends had just pummeled the hell out of me for it, but what did we know?

What is it about unrequited love, anyway? It's a classic problem. I think it tends to happen to the "nice folks" who consider themselves the type that finish last. They don't go after what they want soon enough, and they settle into "love you like a brother/sister" relationships and consider that good enough - any attention is good attention.

I am sure a lot of it has to do with self esteem issues, too. The classic tale of this is either *Bridget Jones's Diary* or Jane Austen's *Sense and Sensibility*. The story starts out with someone who is getting a little "up there" compared to society and feeling some pressure to pair off, and she chooses, utterly, the wrong guy. It takes losing the false pride and gaining the self-confidence to go for the right guy. I know that's true for men seeking women, too.

All I know is that unrequited love can be very, very destructive on someone with delicate sensibilities.

Cut to the summer after sophomore year of college. I'm sharing an apartment with a friend who isn't around and the only friends I have in town happen to be my unrequited love and this guy who is part of my general friend circle (who UL is also a part of), Earnest. The entire summer is spent doing one of four things: hiking, eating ice cream, playing chess, and playing Super Nintendo. Every day, the boys would show up at my place for one of these activities. It was pretty good times.

Anyway, one day, UL is out of town, so Earnest and I go to see a movie. I'm standing in the back trying to find a seat when I feel him totally invade my "friend bubble" and go into "intimacy bubble" in terms of personal space. I am a little weirded out by it, but whatever. I've known this guy long enough; it's not a big deal.

We watch the movie. It's swell. We go home, play some chess, and then I am tired and I want him to leave. This poor guy is a real sweetheart, but he's also fairly dull. He can talk for hours and hours about anything, but I am pretty good about keeping up appearances that I'm interested if I want to be. I'm also still a major tool at this stage, so I don't know enough to just tell him to leave.

So, here's what I do: I get out photo albums of my dog as a puppy. I show him every single photo.

I don't care how much you like dogs, if you can sit through that, something is wrong with you

He was still there.

So then I pull out all the stops and I go into my room and start programming websites. He sits eagerly at the edge of my bed and watches in awe. Something is definitely wrong.

But, hey, I'm 20. I don't know anything.

You're reading this, and I hope you're picking up what I'm putting down. If not, here it is: if someone shows an inordinate amount of interest in your hobbies and doings, beyond logic, even, they are holding a massive, massive secret.

This massive secret is that they think they love you.

You see, in the middle of uploading a file, he clears his throat. "Kristin, I have something I need to tell you."

And you know that tone. That tone that makes you go, "Uh oh. Something is coming that I probably don't want to deal with."

I turn around, "Okay?"

"I like you." I am about to open my mouth, but he puts his hand up, "No, wait. I have wanted to do this forever. Just let me get it out. I like everything about you. Your passion, your kindness, your tenderheartedness. Every moment I'm with you, I can barely contain myself. You're the smartest person I know."

Woah. No one has ever done this for me. And what breaks my heart? I feel nothing.

Earnest goes on, "Remember that time we went kayaking in Oxnard and then drove home together? That's when I knew."

Okay, hold up. I do remember that time we went kayaking. I had been down in Los Angeles and so had the boys. We rendezvoused and met up in Oxnard at my friend's grandparents' place. They had three two-person kayaks. It was me, this guy, three other friends, and UL that day. Which boat did I want to get in? Be my guest. The other friend, however, must have known something was up, because he especially picked UL to kayak with, leaving me with Earnest.

I spent the whole time in my kayak kind of sad I didn't get to be with UL.

Also, the guys' car was jam-packed with stuff, so I ended up taking my kayak partner in my car home. He spent the whole drive up blabbing on and on. I distinctly remember thinking I wish he'd just shut up. I was driving home another friend, who was sleeping in the back seat and I wanted him so badly to wake up and save me from this dullard's conversation.

Don't get me wrong, the guy is sweet, nice, and was a good friend. I just was not really into him, even though he was part of the clique.

And this was the day he decided that I was the one for him.

Finally, when he is done telling me why I am so wonderful, I try very gently to tell him that the feelings aren't mutual. My heart is really breaking for him, because, although I can't tell him, I know exactly how he feels. While he was pining for me, I was pining for someone else.

I hug him good night, and send him home with his thoughts. I figure we're done with that. Oh ho, no.

The next day he shows up again with some flowers. "I didn't get a chance to tell you, your eyes are so beautiful."

"What are you doing?"

"Don't you remember, in the dorms, we were sitting in the cafeteria and you said that if a guy wants you, he has to wallop you over the head and drag you back to his cave? I am not giving up."

I did, indeed, say that. It is, indeed, to this day, also sort of true.

"But, I also have to like that guy, too. We have nothing in common! I don't understand it!"

And we don't. This guy was very frail. He had all kinds of health issues, liked trains, and drums, and was very Christian (and I had recently decided that I was definitively not). He was allergic to my pets. We only spent time with each other when the other guys were around because we seriously did not have anything to connect with.

I told him so. And as I did, I realized that he'd only fallen in love with the idea of me, and not me. How else could you explain it? What he wanted, and what he needed, he wasn't ever going to get from me. And I'd done nothing to lead him to believe that he could.

But nonetheless, he'd held on to this crush for years until it came to a head, and here he was, ready to wallop me and prove that he was the one.

Instead, I had to break his heart.

When UL came back from his trip, he asked where our friend was at - he never came to chess/SNES/ice cream any more. I feigned that I didn't know, and I never told any of our circle about it. One thing about being friends with mostly all guys - you don't really want to mess with the dynamics.

The sad part is that when I broke his heart, he went a bit nuts.

Earnest got into experimenting with drugs. Started running (because I did) and found a girl to go with and then went to town with her. People kept asking me what was up with him, but how was I going to tell them it was over me? And what could I do?

One day, apparently, he was walking around town all high on something and prayed to Jesus to fix him. He was immediately stone-cold sober and from that day on became almost rabidly Christian. He stopped doing anything that wasn't ordained in the Bible, and he moved out of our friends' house because he claimed that it was possessed and he had seen Sodom and Gomorrah in the foggy bathroom mirror while he was showering.

In my book, house possession and foggy Sodom are a bit off the deep end of religiosity. Of course, I shouldn't be one to judge. But the point is: he wildly vacillated from one extreme to the next.

I hope he's okay now. It was hard to respect him after his visions and claims and he started not to spend much time with our clique. People wondered about that change, too, and again, I wasn't going to spill a drop of our secret if he didn't.

I don't pretend to tell you it was me that did this. I am not that fabulous, and was definitely less fabulous back then. It's just a little story about not letting your head run away with your heart, and maybe it's also about the power of the K Mac to turn guys to Jeus.

Hey, at least I don't turn them gay, right?

Kristin Tara McNamara

13 THE ELUSIVE PERFECT MAN

One of the time-tested girl-advices that magazines like Cosmo and Elle tell you is this: always look your best. You never know when that first impression is going to count. You never know when "he" is going to show up. Do you want to lose that opportunity, those vile editors ask; do you want to have that regret?

This is the story of how I found out that there really, really is a perfect ten out there.

What's a perfect ten? Oh, come on. You know the old game - rate the chick/dude on a scale of one to ten. There's a whole website devoted to it.

Oh, you're back? Okay. Anyway. I happen to know, unless things have changed in ten years (because, hah, no way have they), that I am an 8.5.

Why? Because the second weekend of college, a bunch of people, who would later go on to be my core group of friends, and I wandered into the neighborhoods around the dorms and ended up at our very first frat party. While these people stood around with beers, one guy decided it might be a good plan to evaluate the attractiveness of the female companions. They told us to do the same.

About eight guys huddled around, while looking back occasionally at us. I wanted nothing to do with it. Nothing good comes from quantifying someone based on their looks. My roommate and other girl friends from the dorms wanted to know their scores and were told them. The guys respected my wishes and left me alone.

Now, my roommate, who - quite frankly - was a massive, massive bitch, found out what they gave me. And she was pissed. She lauded my score over me for weeks. If I didn't do what she told me to, she would tell me my score.

Well, it turns out, I was a full two points above her, which is why she was pissed. Maybe that's why she spent so much time messing with my poor, naive little head back then.

Dunno.

Okay, back to the story . . .

So, I am pretty happy being an 8.5. I am not as hot as some of my friends, but I ain't ugly either.

Now, when it comes to rating guys, I am very picky. When my friends would play the "who's hotter" game with celebrities, I would always have a hard time.

Brad Pitt? He's maybe a 9. Ed Norton is probably an 8 these days. George Clooney is a 9. Johnny Depp? 9. Christian Bale - ohhh, he's pretty close. I'll give him a 9.5 if he promises to do something nice for your mom tomorrow.

Anyway, so, you see - it's hard for me to find a 10. I think that's partially because for me, you get points for personality. If you are hot, but with a 'tude, you can't score that high with me.

So, as far as I know, there's no perfect ten actor. There's pretty much no hope for a real-life perfect ten, then, is there?

Hah! That is where you're wrong.

It's summer. I am working as a marketing director which has really turned into office-manager-peon-job-that-I-hate-where-the-intern-gets-better-things-to-do-than-me. My boss has already taken me aside and told me I need to dress better for work. Apparently my professional/casual isn't cutting it in an office that gets no visitors and my work is all done on the phone and in front of a computer.

I am wearing some outfit I don't totally love that day - navy blue polo, green flouncy skirt. I might not have taken a shower that morning due to plans to work out at lunch. I am sitting at the downstairs front desk so I look like a secretary. (Nothing wrong with that, but I am The Marketing Director.)

The door swings open. Visitor?

I glance up for a moment and see his dark uniform. Cop?

"Excuse me," he says, breaking into a wide, inviting grin as he leans on the desk and puts his close-shaven face close to mine, "I'm here for the fire inspection.

His black uniform is flawless. His dark hair primly cropped and not strand out of place. His brown eyes blend into the blackest of pupils, dilated of course in the darkened hall, his teeth are white and perfect.

For the first time, ever, and I mean ever, I'm speechless.

He's six feet tall. Wide shoulders, narrow waist. His nametag glistens like the sun.

"Go ahead," I mumble.

I turn on the instant messenger on my computer and text a coworker upstairs, "You are in for a treat."

Okay, so, my office is all women, mostly. The vice president is a man, and he's totally the slimy type salesman you think of who loves terms like "Best Practices" and "Turnkey Solution" and my boss keeps telling me I need to start sounding like him when I talk. What, fake? Ugh.

The rest of the floor is women. They range from mid-thirties to upper fifties.

As this firefighting hunk begins his inspection, the veep pays him no mind, but I notice that although the ladies are on sales calls, the floor goes silent as he passes. Their eyes are riveted. One of them is reddening.

My friend upstairs messages back, "What are you talking about?"

I grin. I think I am blushing, "You'll see."

He goes upstairs. I can hear his feet on the ground above me. There's a muffled conversation with the boss man, and I hear the creaking above. He passes the boss's wife and she makes a curt hello. Then my desk . . . and . . .

"OH MY GOD" is the message I receive. I grin victoriously. The office is totally silent so I can hear his footsteps creaking on the second floor and on down the steps.

He returns to my desk, "Well, all done here. You guys run a tight ship."

I smile, "Oh, we try."

Think of something. Some line. Some move. You can do it.

He leans in again, cocking his head boyishly, "Well, see you next year!"

Next year? Next Year? I feel like Ralphie in *Christmas Story* when he finds out the secret message is "Be Sure to Drink Your Ovaltine." Next Year?

He turns his back, his shirt stretched tight across his lats and shoulders, and like that, the door shuts firmly behind him.

There's a pause. The entire office is silent for a moment.

And then, like in one of those classic scenes from any girly movie you can think of, the girls all converge on my desk, tittering and giggling. We're all blushing. Laurie, the closest in age to me by about five years says, "Kristin, what are you doing? He's your age; you have to go get him!" I'm flattered she thinks I can, even a bit greasy and unkempt as I am that day. We giggle and titter.

My boss comes downstairs. Our faces are flushed, we can't control the elation. He looks amused, like the dad from *Full House* trying to make heads or tails of his daughters. We're nothing but screaming teenagers suddenly.

This man has completely bewitched us. He's beautiful. He's charming. He seems totally unaware of his power.

That is the power of a perfect ten: it's not just pretty to look at, it's show-stopping perfect. I still get bothered when I think about it.

The funny bit is, my friend knows this guy. He comes into his bike shop, and he knows his name and that he's married. That doesn't diminish his power in the least. For this guy, the ring doesn't matter.

I'll admit I have tried to Google stalk him, but he remains elusive. I guess if I really wanted to, I could see him again, but why? That moment will always be perfect and he'll always be my perfect ten.

Oh, man in uniform, we'll always have that sunny day in August. Even when you're horribly disfigured after climbing a tree to save a cat, there is someone in your town that thinks of you and blushes every time.

Kristin Tara McNamara

14 THE WHATCHAMACALLIT

I think one of my biggest problems in dating is that I leave things too ambiguous. As your quintessential "girl next door," I tend to assume that you are hanging out with me because I am one of the guys, and not because you want me "like that." If things start to get weird, or you do something that goes outside my experiences, I start to wonder.

There are those girls who make it plain what the goal is. Then there is me. And it's taken me this long to figure out that I need to quit that.

Anyway, so, like most guys who come into my life these days, this one I met climbing. He contacted me through a website and I was looking for partners, so I figured, "Why not?"

We got along so fabulously, it was scary. He was handsome, he was articulate, he was interesting. We wanted so much of the same things . . . oh, my little heart was skipping a beat.

He also pushed me to climb every single day for a month. I was sore, but it was delicious! I felt myself improving by leaps and bounds. And at the same time, this great guy was slipping into my life and I was getting used to it. But he never made a move.

And, okay, "He's just not that into you," but seriously - why does this guy stay up with me at 2 a.m. doing laundry, teaching me new things, calling me up when he has a bad day - but he's not making a move? Surely he must like me?

Well, it all comes down to one afternoon, a month later. I'm at home, prepping to go to this party with a lot of mutual friends. He calls, all whiny because he can't decide what to do tomorrow and I am busy, and I kind of want to get off the phone so I can blow dry my hair. Whiny whiny whiny. Finally I tell him, "I tell you what, I am hanging up because I need to get ready for this shin-dig, and you can call in ten minutes and let me know what you decide."

And then, as hot wind flows through my strands I think, "No! Take this bull by the horns!"

And I call him up, filled with confidence and bravado: "Get ready. I am coming to pick you up for this party. You will meet someone interesting to go do something with, and it will solve your problems!"

"I can't." Whine.

"Why not?"

"I just can't." Whiiiiiiiine.

"Why not."

"Well, I have to do something with . . . my . . . whatchamacallit tonight."

Oh.

Now, dear readers, what could a "whatchamacallit" be? Could it be . . . his dad? Did the word just slip his mind? His roommate? His dog? No . . . how could you forget with whom you had to something with?

Oh, I know. You forget when you don't want to articulate that perhaps you have a girlfriend.

That's right.

Now, normally, the Kristin would feel like *such* a chump. After all, I never defined the relationship, and he never made a move on me. Of course, it all makes sense now.

Except.

Except that he consciously avoided stating the obvious. No casual, flippant, "girlfriend," no - he called her his "whatchamacallit." He deliberately avoided telling me.

Which means he also deliberately was leading me on, while not doing anything technically "wrong" for a guy in a relationship.

You know, except spending nearly all his free time with me for a month and never coming clean about his chick. I felt really bad for the "whatchamacallit."

He knew he'd done wrong, though. He waited about six months to call me after that phone conversation. And, I earnestly missed him. I let you into my life and a girl gets used to it.

And, a girl even forgives.

But, please, don't "whatchamacallit" me.

Kristin Tara McNamara

15 BAD MRS ROBINSON

When I moved back to San Luis for grad school, I found a very welcoming group of climber guys who invited me out as much as possible. I never wanted for a partner or a weekend filled. It was a great way to come back after leaving a fairly soul-searching summer but one in which I had a close friend for every step of the journey.

I think, however, that this particular group was welcoming not just because I was a climber and new, but because I was a female. You see, in the climbing world, the ratio of true climbing women to men is fairly small. Most girls half-heartedly do it, mainly because their boyfriends want them to. Being a strong, independent-minded gal, that's hard to wrap your head around.

It's also hard to navigate the mating world because of it. Is this person excited because you're a potential partner? And in what way? Romantic? Climbing? And every climber has to admit that they hope to find a partner to share that experience with. I long to meet someone whom I can live with AND road trip with. I want a baby strapped to my back as I trudge out to the base of a climb.

So, sometimes I make the mistake of thinking more of my climbing partner than I should. Sometimes they do the same.

So, a few weeks into grad school, this very handsome, spunky dude invites me on a climbing trip to Bishop (a veritable climbing Mecca on the east side of California) with some of his friends that I know who are actually a bit left over from undergrad. I never made good friends with that crowd as they were a bit younger, but we shared the same rock on many a weekend. I was excited! Back to Bishop! Climbing! New friends!

This guy and I had to leave separately because the other friends were already up there. As we traveled through the desert night, I found I had a lot in common with him and really enjoyed the time we spent together. When we stopped for gas, I went to the beer aisle of the convenience store and looked at him, "Do you think I should bring an offering? What kind do you like?"

He looked a bit sheepish and smiled tightly, "Whatever you think." He seemed against the idea for a weird reason, so I didn't follow through. Besides, I am not a huge beermeister.

We arrived pretty late, but our crew was still up and we had a fun time rocking the Volkswagen van into the wee hours of the morning. As he and I set up our tent for sleeping outside (the van was packed), he noticed that we had pretty much the same sleeping bag. I proudly pointed out, however, that mine was a left-handed sleeping bag I'd got at a discount.

"Left handed?" he mused, "I think, if that's the case, you can mate them together."

"Really?" I asked.

"Yeah! I think so."

As we snuggled into our bags, thoughts of trying to mate the bags together made me wonder if he was, indeed, correct. It could be so fun to see, I thought. I wonder if he's right, I thought.

So, after a few moments in the dark, I sat up and told him I couldn't take it anymore, "We have to do it. I have to see."

Oh man. I am so friggin' naive. A girl tells a guy she wants to mate the sleeping bags and what message is she sending?

Right. Well, I wasn't thinking like that. I was thinking, "Oh! New experience! How awesome!"

So, we got to the business of mating sleeping bags and, as he said, it was a total success. I am thinking that's pretty cool and go to unzip them again when he grabs me and holds me close to him.

Woah, what? What? Well, I am confused, but I am also a tool; if you put me in a situation, I tend to accommodate. Besides, this is a nice guy, he's cute, and even though I'm not ready for anything like that, I let it happen.

So, while I'm snuggled up in his well-muscled arms and listening to him breathe and so freaked I can't sleep, I discover something else about mating sleeping bags: it's insanely hot if one is fully clothed. I spend the entire night spooned into this guy feeling the sweat drip off my back and absorb into my thermal. Lovely.

Morning comes and I am a little awkward about what to do now, but I am thrilled to be out of that position. I pretty much sprint out of the tent and pretend like last night didn't happen.

The rest of the day is fine, but the guy is clearly annoyed at my rejection and brings up random things out of his character like, "We should find hookers out here! I want some hookers!"

At one point, he states: "I need to find a girl my own age."

"Your own age?" I ask.

"Yeah," says our friend. "He's twenty."

Oh, hence the beer. And while I'm only three or four years older than him, the space before and after legal alcohol consumption used to make a big, big difference to me. Oh man. I have done a bad thing.

Either way, he is clearly pissed at me. Or more, he's frustrated. But I don't know what to do. His friends have no idea what happened and frankly, neither do I. And here's this poor, young guy, thinking I am older and worldly and just messing with him. No, I'm not. I am totally clueless. And feeling really uncomfortable. Oops.

That night, as we crawl into our tent again, he says, "Should we mate the bags again?"

"Uh, if you . . . want . . . to."

It doesn't happen.

16 DON'T POKE THE FAT

My mom always says that my problem is that I date climbers. She imagines that climbers are selfish jerks only out for themselves and make bad partners. Funny thing is, I don't really date climbers. You'd think that as a woman who owns and runs a climbing gym with probably 150 eligible bachelors, I would be in heaven, but aside from one guy (whose story isn't funny enough to tell), I have not gotten a single date from the gym.

I do, however, seem to date a lot of cyclists. I think it's mainly because they come to me through friends on the fringe of my groups - always new people to meet that way.

And I have made a pact with myself after going down to the San Luis Obispo criterium (a bike race) last year and seeing that the entire attendance consisted of guys I'd been on at least one date with, even the firefighter serving as a paramedic. And, as someone who is not proud of her record of not being able to find a compatible mate, it was horrifying.

This pact is this: NO CYCLISTS. Perhaps that's because they enjoy biking for hours on end staring at each other's butts. And . . . yeah, that's about it. That's what a road cyclist does. I know. I did it. And then I got kinda bored.

Mountain bikers are different, though. More low key. Not so interested in the minutia. I understand mountain bikers, I think.

Anyway, this is the story of my hanging out with one such cyclist. One who also happens to be a mountain biker, so I decide to violate the pact.

Introduced through friends, I found that he was a perfect foil for my humor. I amused the hell out of myself and others with him around for whatever reason. That had to be a good sign. My friend that introduced us pushed us together.

I wasn't all that into him, but as usual, I was flattered by the interest and happy to see where it went.

The first date was just drinks and nachos. Over these food-type items, I find out that he's roommates with this girl-I-used-to-be-friends-with's boyfriend. Don't ask. It's tawdry girl drama. Let's just say I hadn't seen her in a year or more and was perfectly happy with that resolution.

As the date wrapped up, he asked if I had anything I wanted to do. No . . . did he? No . . . so he ended up driving me over to his place to do.... nothing. So, there we are and he flips on cable and starts watching a concert. Like we are just buds and he knows I'm down. Which I'm not. And it's first date and I am being polite. But, if there's anything I don't enjoy, it's watching concerts on TV.

This is not an awesome date.

Then the aforementioned girl comes home, a little shocked to see me there. I try to make small talk with her while this guy vegs on the couch and she, in typical fashion, can't hang. She makes bitchy comments. The dude makes bitchy comments back. Did I mention that he doesn't like her, either? So yeah, now I am watching a concert, having to negotiate a sticky situation with a girl I'd rather not be around, and listening to them both bicker back and forth.

This is a terrifically awful date.

Finally I am extricated from the situation, I don't remember how, but I am not exactly enthralled by the new dude.

Well, now he's after me to go mountain biking with him. And after a crappy first date like that, where he clearly demonstrates he has no ability to think about my comfort levels, you would think I would say no.

But, here's the problem. I skate this fine line between compassion and toolishness. I try to give people chances. If I am not covered in puke and feces by the end of the night, I will probably give it another go. You never know what you might uncover with time. Or, that's my naive part. I think it's really hard for me to just be callous enough to eliminate people right away - by now I really do kind of know what works and what doesn't, but I want to be nice. I want to give people more faith . . .

So I accept. And accepting a mountain bike invite is a big deal for me. Mind you, he is a professional: he races and wins. His job is dependent on his intimate knowledge of the sport and the mechanics of the bikes. And I? I suck. If you see me around and I have a cut or a bruise, I promise it is from me sucking at mountain biking. I am trying to get better.

But when I do sports, or anything, I don't really like to suck that blatantly. So when I mention to my roommate, who is a federal firefighter hotshot and slogs up mountains hacking things to bits, that I am going running and he wants to come, I tell him no. I don't need anyone but my dog and passing cars to see how bad I suck.

Of course, if you pair me up with someone worse than me, my ego inflates and I perform like a golden god. It's why I like teaching people things . . .

So eventually I cave and agree to go riding with him. And there I am, totally the girl on the bike following the stud. Except this particular stud has a singlet on (a one-piece spandex suit) and has the worst farmer tan ever (I note this as he gets naked to get into it). I am so not turned on. Dudes in spandex are NOT hot. I like mountain biking because it is typically spandex free . . .

When we're done, we agree that Mexican is in the cards and he invites our mutual friend and his girlfriend as well. As we're sitting there, talking and munching on chips and salsa, I do what I normally do: I act silly and entertain people. What can I say? It's a gift.

And another thing I do, which comes from my mind working faster than my mouth, is I flub something up: "So then we take this fart from New York to Los Angeles . . ."

And my dude goes, between snarfing of chips, "Fart? You took a far from NY to LA? HAHAHA!"

And we all laugh at my silly word transposition. I do it a lot.

But he keeps laughing, "You took a fart! HAHAHAHAH!"

Hahahahaha. It's funny, we all get it!

Dinner arrives, but the conversation flows on. My friend is talking about how he's losing weight (and he did, and did a fabulous job of it) and his calves are pure muscle. And, well, because he's my friend, and because I call things what they are, I tell him that a lot of what he's got on his leg is fat.

He must disprove. I must prove. So, I pinch his calf to show him. He responds: "Yowch! I still think you're full of it."

And I can't let it drop, so here's my plan. Since my date is a professional mountain biker, I totally assume he's low body fat, so I grab my own arm, which is admirably stacked with muscle but also sports a nice layer of blubber, pinch it, and show the difference between fat and skin.

To show skin, I pinch small, pull up maybe 1/4 inch, if that. To show fat, I pinch larger and get an inch. "See? Fat versus skin."

And then, to exemplify someone without fat, I go over to my dude and pinch away. And it turns out his arms are totally mushy.

He is softer than me.

Oh man.

Talk about emasculating.

It's not like I set the standard of girlish softness, but come on . . . it's tough to be a guy, an athlete, and still sport more than 25% body fat.

To this day, I'm still blown by it. How you can be fit enough to demolish me on a bike on hills and still have more fat than me is beyond me. And no muscle tone on your arms?

He's still not over my bad word choice and I think the effect is lost on him, "Ha ha ha . . . fart!"

"Dude, I make mistakes. The joke is over."

"You took a fart!"

That's when I realized he wasn't my knight in shining armor.

The next guy I dated, one who actually made it past the first couple dates, got to benefit from this learning experience. One night we were snuggled up in my bed, and I said, "Gee, I am so glad you're not a cyclist."

"Why?"

No reason."

Kristin Tara McNamara

17 MOVIES ARE BAD FIRST DATES

I used to hang glide. I thought I would get hard-core into it until I realized just how prohibitive it is to do that. It's like rock climbing in Kansas. Pointless.

Anyway, the way that lessons work when you start out is that you're given a wing (that's hang glider to the insider), clipped into it with a basic harness, and you start at the top of a gentle hill, not a cliff.

I would take off running down the hill, my wing would catch the air and I'd be lifted off. Beginner hang gliders have wheels on them so that when you land incorrectly, you won't just crash and burn. No, you get dragged. I had these awesome canvas pants that could really take the long distance drags involved. I quickly became the queen of this particular skill. It was actually more fun than stalling the wing and landing properly. I tend to laugh and get hysterical at my own personal failures.

Oh yes, I was a hang-gliding drag-queen.

It drove my instructor nuts so he would try what he could to get me to do it right.

My instructor would always point me to this red flag and tell me to run off the hill to catch the air, and he would go, "That's a sexy, naked fireman! He wants you! Go to him!" This motivation my instructor gave annoyed me. It was so cheesy. I am nothing if not into disproving clichés. Fireman? Please. Firemen can definitely be wonderful hero types, but most of the ones I know are pretty much frat boys that never grew up. Pretty-to-look-at ends being awesome pretty quickly.

But, my quiver is complete in that I have, indeed, dated a firefighter. One date. I flaked on our second.
He wasn't a frat boy; he was an attractive older guy who was a bit meek. I could run at that with a hang glider. I could even crash-land into it.

The plan for our date was to meet for drinks and then check out a movie. A movie I hadn't researched at all. I picked the drink location, and he picks the movie.

I arrive and he's already there - which is cool. Usually I am so prompt, I am first. I hate being first for some reason. There's not many people at the bar so the bartender is chatting with us when I plop down onto the seat and order the bar's signature "Pink in the Middle." It's Chambord and something else and black vodka to top it. It's fun to look at it, and it's a swell conversation piece.

Which, of course works, and we're off.

As we're chatting, the bartender comes up to us again and says, "Hey, I am trying to offload some cookbooks I don't need. Want one?" He sets this stack on the bar and we sort through it. I can't remember what firefighter picks, but clearly, I have to get the *Better Homes and Gardens: Bridal Edition*. It's white, cool looking, and it's the Bridal Edition! How funny is that? How did a bachelor bartender end up with that? I don't ask, and I should have.

It still proudly sits on my shelf. It's funny because it assumes brides have no idea how to cook. I wonder if it tells you about the birds and the bees, too. Obviously, I don't use it a lot.

Anyway, it's time to leave, so we slide off the stools happily buzzing and start crossing downtown to get to the independent film theatre. Double gold stars for this guy for picking the Palm. I like off-beat movies a lot, they are often better than the big-time stuff.

But it's hard to get through the streets. There are people *everywhere*. They're crowded in the street, on the sidewalk. They all look like they are waiting for something. We take a turn, and suddenly we're walking behind three girls bopping around like it isn't freezing out in little hot pants and tank tops. I look past them to see a guy with a big camera filming them, moving backwards. Suddenly I realize we're on some kind of set and I am now an inadvertent extra.

The girls turn to face the huge crowds in the streets and . . . one of them is Lindsay Lohan. Turns out, like many bad movies, SLO has been selected for a scene shooting, and from the looks of it, it's a homecoming parade and all the college kids are pretending to be in high school.

Lindsay, for what it's worth, is not as deathly thin as she was portrayed to be at that time. She looked pretty normal to me. You know, for a Cal Poly Dolly. (The college girls here all look really thin, with bleached out hair, and tan: expensive to keep up.)

The directors to call "action," turning bored looking college students in letter jackets into throngs of dancing, screaming high school kids surrounded by cars inching slowly up the street, painted up with "Go Tigers!" or whatever the fake mascot is. We have to wait for this to be repeated a couple times before we can cross the street to get to our destination. Good thing we left plenty of time to catch previews.

Now, I like surprises, so I encouraged firefighter to keep his choice to himself. He agrees, but admits he doesn't know much about the film himself, just that some of his crew recommended he see it. I'd heard about it from reading the title in the New Yorker a few days ago, but hadn't gotten to reading the description.

The movie that he selected, gentle reader, is *The Aristocrats*.

No, not the *Aristocats*, a cute, family Disney film about kitties.

No, this is about something else entirely. It is comprised of one-hundred comedians involved in telling the same horribly dirty joke in various ways.

As the lights fall, I find I am sitting there next to fire dude as Bob Saget, the sweet little dad from Full House fame tells the story and my stomach is twisting into knots.

I do have my limits. I really don't like potty humor: if you talk about farting, pooping, peeing, or puking, I'm out of there. This movie was all about that. The entire time I am thinking that his fire crew must really, really hate him.

I am pretty sure firefighter guy is horrified. I mean, both of us would probably have enjoyed the film for our own reasons had we not been total strangers wondering if this was leading toward an amorous relationship. It's kind of hard to laugh at things like that if you have no idea what the other person is thinking. It was even harder to walk out of the theatre at the end. What do you do? "Good movie?" "Best movie ever?" "I liked the one about the pig fucking the four-year-old daughter?" I mean, really.

There's a moral here. I think it's research the movie you pick for taking a girl on a first date to. And besides that, movies are stupid first dates.

18 KNOWING WHAT YOU WANT CAN BE SCARY

My roommate and I lauded the quality of single guys in town a little too often one day, so we decided to start trying to find ones in different circles. Perhaps we were going wrong by dating schlubs, average Joes, and I must admit I don't have a single white-collar success under my belt.

Happy hour, happy hour must have single men, right? We tried the expensive bars, perhaps we could find some accountants or lawyers or something.

Turns out, no, happy hour attracts one thing: old couples. We hit up all the hot spots. Old couples. It's like they feel safe while the college crowd is pre-partying, so they can go to the spots they used to twenty, thirty years ago.

"That's it!" I declare. "I am trolling places for dudes! I am now *that* girl! There is only one way to go from here!"

And where do you go? You go to the Internet. It's time to own it. Be unashamed in it. After all, how many people have told me that "So-and-so found their significant other on the Internet." Okay, fine. So I will openly declare that I am single and what I want. Perhaps it cuts to the chase. I will know straight off what they want, and they will know what I want.

I make it really, really clear. My heading is "Looking for a Healthy, Long Term Relationship."

Of course, this still nets some awesome wackos:

For instance, when you write a missive (and you know I would), and the response a guy feels like sending you is - "how are you?" Not a winner.

And there's the one that, ladies, never touch:

"So, curiosity has got me here, and not sure if I'll be back. Not even sure why I'm writing you, curiosity? Maybe, but really wanted to give you props for putting yourself out there and writing such an excellent portrait of yourself. Nice work. Such a good image of who you are and what you're looking for. Not really in a good place right now to pursue this, but maybe in a few months...but if I was, you would definitely be someone to get to know. Oy vey, one too many tonight . . ."

Oh, so basically you're in a relationship you might break off pretty soon, you are pursuing me, and you're drinking? Good plan.

Or: "well what ive read about u so far intrieges me,im 26 6'0 195p and im very fit and athletic.i live in slo and there isnt much out here!!!i luv 2 go out but no one 2 good looking???????"

Spelling totally only counts if you use more than fifty words in your response. Also, bonus points for not making a lick of sense.

And then, possibly my favorite?

"I am happily married (14 yrs this summer) to a wonderful woman who is a lot like your description of yourself. We're both 37 but pissed that 27 seems like yesterday. So why was I reading the personals in the first place? Well, we're looking for a girlfriend to share. Not a serious relationship, but casual, comfortable and possibly long term . . . So far it has been impossible to find someone that has any interest in such a relationship that isn't an outright swinger or weirdo, and that is definitely not what we're after."

Yeah, sounds AWESOME. Sign me up.

Or the simple, "How about i just lick your wet spot until the sun rises"

I mean, damn. You want all types? You got all types. I also got something like sixty or seventy replies.

I did get a couple promising replies, but only one or two dates out of it. This particular guy replied with a phrase I desperately hate, "What up." And I now say it sarcastically but it's become so trite, I don't think people know it. He seemed interesting enough, so I chatted with him over instant messenger and he was utterly charming. Despite him not at all being my type, I thought, why not?

For our first meeting, I gave him an assignment, since he lived in an area I wasn't very familiar with: find something to do in the area that introduces me to it. I'll meet him after work.

And when I do, he tells me to get in the car; we're going to the butterflies. He's brought his camera. As soon as I get out of the car, he rubs the small of my back. So obviously, the guy is interested.

Now, I feel kind of bad, because I have seen the butterflies a lot. There's a spot of eucalyptus trees along a strand of beach in Pismo that monarch butterflies migrate to. They come in droves and spend the winter there, thousands of them. So many of them that they weigh the tree branches down and swarm so tightly they look like the gum tree's leaves unless you look closely. I think it's cool, so I go all the time - but I didn't tell him that and it's a pretty good idea if I had no idea about it, so I down play that as he sets up the camera and painstakingly takes a few shots. I act totally interested up to a point. The tripod and camera is really a bad third wheel to drag along on a first date.

Now he tells me we're going down the path to the beach. I kick off my shoes and climb this tree. He follows me right up, and I find out he climbs. At least a little.

As the sun sets, he sets up his camera and starts taking oodles of photos. I tell him the shots he's getting are going to turn out crappy (I know these things), but he does it anyway, so I am really, really bored.

I have also chosen this really gross spot with some kind of rotting food right there, but for some reason, I feel like I can't move. Like, if I shift nearer to him, that's too much in my space. And if I move away from it, then I'm being a bit rude and being too closed with my signals. Yes, I think about these things. He's taking photos, and I am planted there in the sand next to what could be puke.

We sit there for a long time. I'm bored.

Finally I stand up, trying to suggest it's time to go, and he grabs my leg and starts to run his hand up and down it, "Oh, big calves, eh?"

Yeah . . . never mention how big a girl is, unless she is clearly a body builder and tries. My calves are very big - I'm not entirely sure why they are, but they always have been. I am a stacked chick. But you don't have to point out how huge I am. that's like the writer I met at a climbing expo who was like, "Your forearms are bigger than mine!" Yah! I am huge! Go me!

Anyway . . . he grips my calf and says, "What's the hurry?"

"Nothing, I'm just a little bored is all."

"Well, the sun is setting. I have an idea," he says, looking up at me.

"Oh yeah?" I say, feeling pretty uncomfortable.

"Yeah, I think you should kiss me."

"Uh . . . "

So now, you have to understand something. Lots of people just give kisses away like advice. I am a lot more reserved than that. There are too many guys who think that a kiss is deserved, but it is because of this, that I have never really liked kissing. I happen to be one of those people that needs an emotion behind a physical expression to feel it.

But he's up and he just goes for it. To his credit, I guess it didn't suck, but it didn't make my knees buckle, either. I mean, well, welcome to the ultra cliché - kissing at a beach sunset. It was ballsy and I gave him points for it. It also cut right to the chase that usually scuttles things for me: leaping from friends to intimacy. I mean, it was pretty clear where this was going to go. And that made me a lot less uncomfortable.

I agreed to go to dinner with him and over Thai food, he starts telling me what he thinks of me: he's been keeping a mental list. He shares it. Tough, impulsive, big calves, smart, and impatient.

You know, that's one thing I hate about dating. People make snap judgments about you. It also makes me really re-evaluate how I am and how I see myself. So that's good, I guess, but this guy had no problem just flat out telling me his impressions of me.

And of course, most of the qualities he listed were circumstantial. I was "impatient" because I didn't want to drag out the communication via email forever and because I thought I'd gotten lost on the way to his house. And because his photography bored the hell out of me. I was impulsive because I was just in that mood.

And he was keeping a list. I know I am neither impulsive nor impatient. At least not in my head. I didn't need to be told these things.

I had to be like, "Do you do this to your friends?"

"Do what?"

"The list."

"Oh, no."

"So why do you think I'd like it?"

"Oh." And he quit. But, dude, I am not impatient.

After that, he mentions he wants to see a movie and I think that's fine, so off we go. As we're sitting in the theatre, he makes his move, and his arm is around me. This is entirely new to me. I do not do this crap with a total stranger. I don't do it with any of my guy friends, even ones I've known for years. I don't even do it with my siblings. It is hard to concentrate on the movie because it's so weird to me.

I decided to go with it and lean into him. We do that for a bit. It's nice, I guess. I feel kind of secure and cozy. It's nice that he's into that. I have friends who would rather sleep on the floor than with a girl in their bed with them. I guess it shows he's capable of these things. That's nice.

I decide it's okay. I decide maybe my guard can be dropped.

And then he . . . he kisses me on the top of the head.

What what what?

Okay. I kiss my dog on the top of her head. Maybe when I was five, my dad kissed me on the top of my head. I do my characteristic nervous giggle. I guess he interprets that as appreciation and does it again throughout the show.

And I have no idea what to think. It seems like a very intimate, sweet, disarming thing to do. And you do it when you know someone. How is it he's known me for only a couple hours and he's moved to head-kiss?

This guy is either really, really open or he is really, really weird. Or I am a hardened woman. And really, it could be none, or all three. This is where I make a call: yay! Finally a man who is open to such things, or . . . wow, this is a manipulative guy who is a little needy . . . or something.

When the movie is over, I leap up, and walk straight to my car ahead of him. I need a little control back.

When we get back to his place, he tells me he has a CD he wants me to have and hands it to me as I get into my truck to leave. Things like that make me also go, "Woah." I am very careful in early relationships to not make any assumptions about seeing someone again. Most especially not giving them my stuff.

And then he goes in for the goodnight kiss, which he gets because, I mean, we're already into that stage. What's another?

And as he walks back into his house, I am in a bit of a panic. What the HELL just happened? This guy just gave me his CD, assuming he's got even a short future with me, he kissed me within an hour of knowing me, and . . . he kissed the top of my head. Repeatedly!!!

He's got to be a freak! I need to get out of here.

My keys. Where are my keys. My keys . . .

I dig in my purse. No keys.

I look around the seat. No keys.

Shit. I think I left them in his house.

And I do not want to go back in there. In fact, I never want to see him again. That was just too weird. I cannot deal. That was hours upon hours of really getting out of my personal comfort zone.

But how do I leave? What do I do?

Ah hah . . . your Kristin always goes prepared: I have a spare key in my car. I take it out, start the car up, and drive home.

Dude, he kissed me on the head! On the head!

Of course, you know . . . I am still not free. I still have my keys at his house. Like, my work keys. My house keys. I think about changing locks briefly. I can't just ask him to mail me them. Oh no, I have to go back. I have . . . to . . . go back.

You know that he thinks I left them on purpose. That's how the game is played. But here I am trying to think of every possible way to get them back without crossing paths with him again.

I was able to stay away a week and make do with the spares I had, but well, I did end up going back.

And there we are in his kitchen, me telling him that I couldn't stay long (because I was freaked out and didn't want to stay long). "Well, make time for me, because I really like you."

And, being ever so tactful, I said something like, "You think?"

This becomes one of the "dating stories" I tell my friends I rarely see when we run into each other at the market. We all have a good laugh.

But, well, the joke's on me because he ended up "sticking." It was not the most fun to introduce him, my friends knowing full well that he'd been chalked up to another bad date that we all laughed at.

He did really like me, and eventually he convinced me to go back. And I gave him a real chance, but only after I told him what a tool he was like on our first date. What can I say, he took my criticism well. That's always the first sign of a keeper.

By the way, I think he'd be quick to tell you I am one of the most patient people he knows. So there!

19 KILLER DATING

The year is 2005 and I am about a month out from taking my comprehensive exam to get my Master's degree. I am one of the more active students in the program, I know my stuff, and I've been diligent in the study group with my friends.

Along comes the Doc. I honestly don't remember how I met him except that I know it wasn't in person. Perhaps it was during my little go at Match.com or something. He seemed to be pretty much anything a girl like me could ask for: smart, athletic, goofy, fun. He'd recently moved to SLO to start residency at one of the hospitals in town in the emergency room. His last name was so ironic, it wasn't funny: we'll call him Dr. Murder and that about hits it.

Dr. Murder and I had fabulous phone chemistry and despite my being way too busy to pursue anything (and less than busy, more preoccupied with the test coming up), I figured we should meet up, which we did.

He turned out to be a very neat guy. Not really my 'type' per se (I somehow end up with tall, lanky guys, and he looked to be an ex-high school linebacker), but I know that from past experience, "type" means nothing in the scheme of things.

The one thing I just could NOT get over was his belt o' gadgets.

Let's take a little break here. The Kristin? She is a total nerd. She likes reading and playing the freerice.com game that tests her word skillz. She programs HTML for fun. She trains dogs to do precise commands. She over thinks everything and . . . yes, she is definitely a nerd.

But there's this fine line, friends, between the nerd and the geek. Geeks? Man, geeks scare you. Geeks have closets full of Dungeons and Dragons paraphernalia, they LARP on Saturday Mornings at Santa Rosa Park, they may or may not live at home still, and they have every techno gadget available.

And rather than carrying them in pockets, they holster these gadgets on belts that make them look like the geek wing of the SWAT team.

For me, that is the ultimate turnoff.

That is saying a lot. I mean, I used to be a tech support rep. I spent my college years hanging out with engineering geeks. My junior prom date reportedly denies asking me to go with him. I tried to teach myself Japanese so I could read manga (Japanese anime comics) in its original language.

Yet, I'm sorry, but I think I'm better than the belt-geek militia.

It is one of those things I could struggle to get over, but . . . well.

So time goes on and he keeps calling me to hang out. Dr. Murder is persistent and I'm flattered. I mean, a doctor! I rule.

But honestly, I really was stressed about the exam. He was so kind, "Okay then, come over, sit in my garden and study and I won't even bother you. Let's just spend time together."

So kind. Still a geek. I said no.

Eventually he gave up.

Time passed and I failed the exam, plummeting my self-confidence into the depths of the darkest well. Still licking my wounds, I'm at the dog park one day and he shows up with a cute, svelte blonde and a Weimeraner.

It turns out he married her. Not six months from our little . . . whatever it was. They have a beautiful baby.

And you have to wonder, what if I had gotten over his sling-belt full of electronics and thrown caution to the wind. It's not like my prudence helped me pass the exam. Would I be Mrs. Dr. Murder?

Kristin Tara McNamara

20 DON'T TALK TO STRANGERS

So, there's something I really, really enjoy doing when I have some free time and access to the Internet. I peruse Craigslist. I like looking at what I can get for free, what jobs might be out there, and far less innocuously, I like looking at the "casual encounters" in all their risqué' glory.

The fact alone that people post photos of their penises fascinates me. Moreover, I cannot believe the things these people propose. I always wonder about the logic of it, too. If one were to, say, answer one of these posts, how does that work? Do you just show up at someone's door and go at it? Can people do that? No consideration for build up or privacy or awkward encounters later on? And what do people say to one another on initial contact?

Beyond that, I like looking at the personal ads, too. Men for women, women for men, women for women, men for men. Honestly, it really makes me feel a little down about humanity. What people want, what they think they can get, or what little they expect, it's just plain sad. There's never once been a personal ad on craigslist that made me feel like responding. They are usually like, "Hi, I am looking for a girlfriend. I like to laugh and have a good time. Must be disease and drug free."

Woo, please, please, I am SO excited to meet this one! I mean, we have so much in common! I, too, like to laugh and have a good time! And the man's got standards! He doesn't want diseased, druggie ladies! He must be a catch!

So, one time, I saw kind of a plaintive little post on there. It was about this guy who was so shy with girls he just wanted experience. He came off as very insecure and afraid and it tugged at my heart strings. I wrote him a letter and told him very clearly that I didn't want to date him, but I did want to talk to him a little about this.

We had a nice little chat on the Internet. I told him that we all have our insecurities, and that women aren't special, ethereal creatures. I told him that I, too, am shy on the approach and I find it hard to make eye contact with hotties in public places. I told him not to fret - read some books, practice things, and if you aren't feeling attractive, walk around downtown and note how many people look at you - we look at attractive people and ignore those we don't like to look at, even for a moment.

Anyway, the conversation naturally ended and I was happy. The deed had been good.

Except, maybe a month later, I get this phone call at 9 pm on a Friday night. I'm at home, studying for some grad school type thing, and it's a number I don't know, so I answer it.

"Hi, this is the guy you talked to about dating." Oh, great. I never gave him my number, but being that I'm easily Internet findable . . .

"Uh, hi."

"I have a proposal. Come out with me. Right now. Let's have a silent date. We don't talk."

It's Friday night, 9 pm. I am not allowed to talk? What? I didn't ask for this.

"Uhh, thanks, but I'm busy right now."

Pause.

He comes back with an angry tone, "Look, you wanted to help me get over being shy, the least you could do is go out with me."

"Dude, I don't want to. I am busy."

"You said you were shy, quit being shy and go out with me, dammit."

"How did you get my number?"

"Internet."

Obviously.

"Look, I don't want to go out tonight. I have plans and that's that."

"Okay, well, can I keep your number and call you again to go out?"

Now, here's the defining moment, the moment I know that I've finally learned: I say, "No, I would rather you didn't." In the past, I would have been a polite tool, told him "sure," and just not returned his calls.

"Fine, you bitch!"

Harrumph! Guess he wasn't so shy after all!

Kristin Tara McNamara

21 THE KISS RAPE

I really, and truly, do not know what my problem is. I think most people would agree that I am not overtly sensual in how I present myself: it's mere accident that I take a sexy shot or my eyes glaze over into something approaching "bedroom." So, tell me this: why am I frequently the victim of what I like to call "kiss raping?"

To set this up, you need to know that I am someone who really, really likes to dance. When I was in college, I used to stand in the dorm room window and rock out for the boys in the dorm across the road. They'd call up and request songs. And get your mind out of the gutter. I'm talking about really flailing and acting stupid dancing. Nothing involving poles or boas.

As I've gotten older, I tend to be happy to dance just about anywhere. Sometimes that embarrasses my friends, but it seems to make people who don't know me very amused - and I am definitely one who enjoys amusing strangers. I don't even require alcohol at this point to get me warmed up.

So, there I am, in a swarm of moving, sweaty bodies, just giving it a go and really enjoying myself. Shake-shake-shake that butt, do a little two-step, swing your arms around, etc. And all of a sudden, there he is.

You know that guy: he watches you from afar and decides you're easy or something and he comes up behind you and then grabs you when you're not looking and attempts to dance with you. Now, if you are not of my generation or younger, you need to understand that this is not exactly the waltz. Lots and lots of people enjoy "freaking" with one another, which is basically simulated sex to music. It can be as serious as you want it to be, and for me? Dude, I just wanted to dance.

One thing I wish I've cultivated in my years is the slap. I think that the way of the slap may have gone out with gloves and revolvers, but when a guy sidles up to you, never even gives you a glimpse of what he looks like, doesn't introduce himself, and then attempts to rub his private parts on your leg - well, he deserves a slap.

That kind of thing can probably get me into trouble

The way I handle it? I roll my eyes at my friends and if I'm lucky, one of my guy friends will start freaking me in front, which is the incredibly classy way of saying, "May I cut in?"

It reached a new low, however, on my brother's birthday in Santa Barbara one year. We all went out dressed in full St Paddy's day regalia (his birthday is March 17) and tore up the dance floor. My brother is in his forties and so are all of his friends, so you would think I would be immune to the freaking, but no such luck. Some guy attaches himself to me and as I'm trying to extricate myself from the situation . . . he spins me around, grabs my head, and proceeds to try to make out with me.

I mean, yuck!

And he's got my head in a vice grip so there's no way I can get out of it without kneeing him in the crotch. I twist and twirl my way out of that situation and run to my bro, who is definitely not the kind to beat anyone up, and when I tell him what happens, he just shouts, "What? WHAT?" (it is really loud).

Well, it happened again on my recent vacation. I'm out with friends, rocking out to this funny 80s cover band, and not a single dude attempts to freak. They all stand respectfully back as our group, mainly made up of husbands and wives, cut a rug.

Well, as I'm going up the stairs of this Irish pub (and I do mean Irish, the guys were straight from ol' Erie) to de-sweat and take a break, the one bloke stops me and tells me I look fabulous. Ha ha. No I don't. I am sweaty, a bit over my normal weight thanks to weeks of good eating and under exercising, and I've got no makeup or hair coiffing to speak of. "I been watchin' ye all night," he brogues, "an ye's the prettiet in the entire bar." Flattering to say the least, but I'm on a mission so I thank him and try to get up. He grabs my hand, "Come have a drink w'me."

"Oh, I can't."

"Why not?"

"I'm here with me friends." (Have I mentioned I take on accents really easily?)

"Aww. Jest one drink?"

"Naw, yer too rich for my blood!"

Well, fine then."

He leans forward and puckers his lips. Oh well, I think. He's drunk (I'm not), and it is flattering to have an attractive brother of my homeland want a little peck. And so, I gift him it.

Bells clang in my head - my mom has always said, "You watch the Irish - they're charming, like the Italians. Can't trust them." See, Mom deep down is kind of pissed she fell for my dad's wiles. She's always saying how no-good the Irish are.

Anyway, throughout the night, whenever I steal away, the same thing gets repeated, only the puckers are more forceful every time and I refuse them.

When the lights finally go up, and the owner of the bar concludes the evening with a lively rendition of an old, long Irish rebel song (which I know and merrily sing along), another Irishman comes up to me from behind and says hello. Asks me what I'm doing tonight (not going home with you, that's for sure) and I tell him I'm in from out of town. I tell him where I'm from and he rewards me with a story about getting into an accident down in Santa Maria. He asks what I do there for a job, and I simplify it by telling him I'm a college professor.

"Ach! I'm honored, I am." And he grabs my hand and kisses it. That's a first. I am tickled. Damn, the Irish charm.

He says that despite the distance, he wonders if he can't call me sometime, if I have a card. Well, I do happen to have one, and I figure the hand kiss earns him a card (and heck, if he does happen to call, I have more fodder, eh?). As I pull it out of my wallet, he goes, "Jaysus, Kristin Tara McNamara? That's a beeutiful name."

Hah! I know!"

We get into a farewell embrace, but he seems to be holding out for something, so I kiss him on the cheek. Oops, bad move. He goes in for a kiss, and before I know it, he's grabbing my head and his tongue is rimming my lips. The whiskey and cheap beer is melting my senses. His lips are cold and probing. Yegads!!! I pull away and he won't let me. Turning my head way as he slobbers on my cheek, unwilling to give up the ghost, I finally get out of it.

And then I slap him.

Or that's how I wish it had gone.

In all honesty, I brush it off and tell him my friends are ready to go and I am the driver, and see ya.

"You'll answer if I call?" he asks.

"Yep." I say, totally, utterly lying.

::shudder:: I am pretty sure my friends see this all and I am worried they think I am something of a little trashy skank now, especially after I gave him my card. But come on - how was I to know?

But it does make me wonder . . . is it better to fall for the charms of an Irishman who goes after what he wants or is it better to play the games that come with a shy guy who never figures it out? And what is it about my reserve that utterly falls away when I leave my hometown?

Kristin Tara McNamara

22 FACEBOOK: IT'S COMPLICATED.

So one of my good friends and I had a late-night conversation about how weird the whole "relationship with" feature is on social network sites. I have decided to avoid it altogether by not filling it in, because, well, I'm mysteriously like that. He was like, "You're right, it's *commiting*."

Which it is. Totally. But moreover . . . I have to find out people are getting married and engaged from Facebook announcements lately and that is ever so wrong.

But apparently, I come to find out, breaking up is the worst because when you change your relationship status, it asks you to confirm it, right? So say you break up with your lady love and you get home and in this day and age she's already deleted you from her friends list and requested the notification. You are now in a relationships with . . . nothing!

Nice!

So during our conversation, he agreed to marry me on Facebook. And not an hour later, he then got cold feet and decided an Open Relationship was better since the distance is a factor (he lives on the east coast). And then . . . the he broke up with me. I can't catch a break. Vile, vile man - thousands of miles can't shield him from breaking a girl's heart.

Anyway, despite running the gamut of emotions lately because of that horrible younger man, I'm doubly horrified by Facebook's "in a relationship" feature now. I think I will run the litmus test soon and ask all of my friends to be in a relationship with me.

Why is there no polygamy feature?

23 TELEPHONE GAME

Do you know where the phrase, "Jump in the sack" originated? I do. It's one of those gems you learn when you're an English grad student. And you thought I just read good.

Here's how it went down: back in the day, people didn't all live in cities and have cars, and the towns were so small that basically you were looking at incest if you had your eyes on your next door neighbor. People would walk and walk to church socials and hootenanies, and what have you. They'd meet, make eyes, maybe wrap a ribbon around the maypole - you know, really dirty stuff.

And then, there'd be that spark.

And frankly, I am still flabberghasted. Here we are in the digital age and I very rarely feel that spark, even though I encounter hundreds and hundreds of people in a week.

I remember driving through Kentucky backwoods with a friend on a climbing trip and seeing people in real, honest-to-goodness hovels with tires piled high. They'd be sitting on their decrepit porches like two happy clams. How did they meet? And I quoth the Southerner, Mr. Jones: "Kristin, in my town there are the Jones and the Smiths. And if I hadn't got out of town, I'd have had to go with the Smith. Incest is NOT a lie." Ahhhh, good to know.

Anyway, so our fair maiden would catch the eye of a ranch hand without even a horse to call his own, much less a Model T, and he would take off from dirty hard work in the coal mines and walk one hundred miles (or five hundred, if you're the Proclaimers) just to be the one to fall down at her door (tell me you get this joke).

Well, she'd be tickled pink, and her parents, wanting to offload the dead weight, would escort her to the conversation chair for chaste bonding time. This chair is basically your standard wooden chair with arms, but point one in one direction and one in the other direction, with the armrest presenting a handy spacing feature allowing for the two awkwardly chatting youngsters' desires not to touch eachother.

Well, it would quickly be time for the whole family to go to bed, so to encourage the natural bonding process, and because it would be really mean to send the young chap back out into the darkness and the dreaded diseases and evils that lurk in it, they'd take a burlap bag and sew him into it so just his head stuck out. He'd be lying down in the same bed with our young lass, but could not so much as get up to take a pee.

Oh yes, spend all night sweating in a burlap sack, unable to move or itch or do anything, but next to the woman you love. A man could not *wait* to *jump into the sack*. And thus the phrase began. Ironically, the current phraseology reflects the complete opposite of the sack's objective.

Anyway, back in the day, the guy really had to work for the girl. All that walking, talking, and sack sweating really tested the mettle of a man.

And yet today, we have telephones. Hooray.

Now a guy can flatter you by asking for your phone number and if you're sprung enough, make you wait by the phone for eons. It's wonderful.

Or, a girl can call at any time of the day, all day, just to see what you're up to. This is otherwise known as "unhealthy stalking."

Where is the work? Where is the mettle testing? Gone, gone with the wind! Just dial a number. And heck, thanks to programming, you don't even have to remember the digits, much less her name.

So, being a massive tomboy, I do not like phones. Granted, when I was younger, I loved them. I loved getting calls because it meant I was cool. I remember when Jimmy Joe called me that time in Junior High and utterly faked being interested in dogs for an hour just to talk to me. I was so cool! Or running to catch the phone before my mom did so I wouldn't have to be embarrassed in high school that – gasp – I lived with my *parents*!

And then I grew up and started realizing that most phone calls weren't that fun. So, yes, okay, sometimes I screen my calls. Not because I hate you, but because I am just so NOT in the mood to talk to you.

Now, there are all these rules to dating and phones. Don't call right away or you'll seem to eager. Girls, hang up first. Blah blah blah. Generally the maxims have good rationale behind them, but when you like someone, you ignore the reasons and think, "My, it's so refreshing that someone is willing to break the Dating Rules!"

Or I do. I am quickly realizing the correct reaction should really be, "My, this is a red flag for a psychological issue." Sad. Yet still, I maintain my naive faith that "this one" is different.

Enter Dog Park Guy. (Oh, another one, you say - I told you . . .) Met in the usual way: Fury decides he's cool, drops the ball at his feet, he picks it up, throws it, repeat - Instant Conversation Starter. My dog is such the pimp. With that, my usual 20 minute fetch-fest with the mutt managed to stretch into a two-hour one. That's usually a good sign. He's quite a bit older, but he's interesting and kind of cocky (which is something I tend to mistake for confidence, but yeah).

As I drive away, I'm disappointed that I won't see him again, but I do! It turns out that he's a very competitive cyclist (and I've had quite enough of these, thank you), and as such, he frequents places I do. It didn't take long for him to crop up. I ask a mutual friend what his story is: recently broken up with serious girlfriend, looking for more, and through my intercessor, Dog Park Guy finds out I'm interested and calls me up.

And talks and talks. Cool, I think. I hang up. A few hours later, he's back. Again? Well, I guess this guy knows what he wants! Go him! Break those rules!

We get to hanging out, I go over to his house to watch that crab fishing TV show that's on late at night, and no move is made (oh, are we seeing a pattern here?). I run into him on my bike and we go to lunch. Meet up for a dog play date.

Nothing happens. Except, thinking about it, he did pat my head once. So, clearly, the chemistry isn't there.

So why is it that he's calling me two, three, four, five, six times a day?

I'm on this softball team and he wants to talk to me before, during, and after a game. I suggest he comes out to watch instead of calls, but he doesn't.

He has to go away for a week to Wisconsin. He calls me late at night, drunk and filled with bratwurst. "I wish you were here, you'd be having so much fun with me." Awww.

He gets back, and we arrange to meet at the dog park. He gets there and instead of sitting next to me on the bench, selects a completely different one, meters away. He's awkward. Conversation is bad. Say what?

We both end up in San Francisco one night and we go out to one of my favorite Irish pubs with one of my best friends. I am smashed. He is smashed. It's late. Suddenly we three find ourselves on a beach together. My friend wanders off. Before I know it, he's hugging me from behind, watching the moonlight lap the ocean crests and valleys. I breathe in . . . finally, finally . . . and . . . nothing. He lets go and backs up slowly, "I think we should find your friend."

We spend the night in his hotel room, but my friend and I share a double bed he has as a spare. We say goodbye in the morning, grab bagels, and head off. My head is filled with that stupid chemical that produces excitement, twitterpations, along with a killer hangover headache, and other such nonsense. Soooooooo close.

He calls twice that next day.

This, my friends, is what we call "Feeding the Beast." Give me just enough to keep me guessing and I'm yours forever. I am that stupid.

Finally, I have had enough of this phone palling. I give him one final shot: call him up, invite him out to a live show, and no - he can't. He has to go to bed. At eight p.m. He would rather sleep than hang out with me. It's stupid, it's ridiculous, and I quit playing the game.

The phone calls peter off after I start screening. I'd sit there, looking at the phone as he called five times a day, just plain wondering - what is up with this guy? Does he just like phones? Did he like me, but he just couldn't deal in real life?

Dunno.

Kristin Tara McNamara

24 TEXTING: THE UN-TOOL

Back in the day, we had walking. Then, Mr. Graham Bell gave us telephones. And then, in the early 90s, we all got Prodigy and AOL and suddenly there was email. We went from interpersonal relations to verbal to text. We did okay. People figured out pretty quickly not to put things in writing they'd regret.

And then, and then we got text messaging.

Okay. So, let's take a step back.

I think most people would agree that I am not shy. I have an opinion; I will share it with you. I will do it abrasively if that is what amuses me or if you can take it. I call it "Kristin Tough-Love." Too many people say things in a roundabout way, and when I finally came out of my shell, I realized it's better to just get it out there.

That's why I lead a workshop on diversity awareness this week for the full-time faculty. They ate it up. "Well, what do I do when I talk about scientific evidence suggesting that homosexuality."

I interject: "Homoeroticism. It's a tendency, not an action . . ."

"Uh, okay. When it suggests there's a natural, genetic element. That makes my Christian students cringe."

"Well, maybe they ought to cringe a little. Thinking and challenging dogma can hurt. Why are you trying to make the classroom safe? The world isn't safe."

Oh yes, my professors ate it up, and they laughed at all my jokes. They asked me for a "part two" next year. The sad irony is that I am telling people above me, who are paid more, enjoy more benefits and respect, how to teach. But I still can't even get an interview for a full-time job as a professor.

Le sigh.

Anyway. My big point in this is that I think a lot of people assume I am upfront about everything.

That's a big no.

I am not so good about dealing with really intense personal emotions. That usually does not get brought up in classrooms so I've been safe so far.

For example, in college I happened to discover that people really did just like to screw with you for no reason. I was a lot less caustic then and my dorm roommate did a good job of not playing fair and telling me to like it. The only way I was able to deal with it was to instant message her. We'd sit there with our backs to each other, in the same room, having serious, serious conversations on IM. Simply because I couldn't verbalize how I was feeling without crying. I think she played along because she found it immensely funny how much I wanted to pour my heart out to her while she did everything she could to undermine me. And I took it because I had to share a room with her. Pretend everything is all right!

Oh yes, I was a sad sack.

I still find it hard to express really deep emotions to people. My preferred method is via letter or email. If you haven't noticed yet, I write better than I speak, and I have time to edit everything from grammar to diction. Even then, even if I'm trying to declare my love to someone or something, I leave it subtle and ambiguous, "I think you're the aces."

Dude, what guy can't read between the lines of that particular gem?

It's something I'm working on.

So, let's say I'm in a relationship with someone and I really had a great time with the guy: I am probably not going to adequately express that to him at the time. I'll say something like, "That rocked! Go you!"

And then, give me a day or so to think and I will produce an eloquent, suitable-for-framing love letter of appreciation.

Of course, the guys I tend to date don't actually appreciate this, which is really a waste.

One particular beneficiary of my letters did me one better, and never responded to them. I would send my deepest feelings out into the void and get nary an acknowledgment. Old Kristin would have gone nuts, but I have come to see that one thing that you have to do to be truly loving is not have expectations. It is enough that *you* love and that *your* heart is open, I think.

During a conversation once, I kind of brought up that it was kind of weird he didn't respond, to which he nobly said, "Well, knowing you, you are doing it without wanting anything back. I was kind of thinking if I did that, it would cheapen the experience." So, okay. I continued sending my belated love into the chasm, with the understanding that it was appreciated.

He was pretty good verbally. Had no problem expressing himself. I suppose he thought it was a tolerable aspect of my personality, but he probably didn't find it enchanting.

But once we broke up, the guy had no problem expressing himself through writing. Via text.

I had told him that although I loved him dearly, I couldn't see any good of maintaining contact with him. He had done well by me, I had done well by him, but enough inconsiderate things had happened in between that I knew I didn't need that in my life anymore. He was really upset about this, telling me he didn't know how I could possibly just cut him out like that and how I had so positively affected his life in every way. I would also like to point out that technically, he was the one dumping me in this conversation.

Patiently trying to explain it without dashing his ego to bits, I asked him to let this conversation be our last. He promised to respect my wishes but told me he'd be around if I ever changed my mind.

Well, a month later, he still hasn't returned some of my stuff, which I really needed. I didn't want to just go into his place and take it (I know he hadn't changed the code) but the thought did occur to me. I definitely didn't want to call him. Email would be too much of an open for conversation. What to do . . . what to do . . .

Ahh, the passive-aggressive text.

I was really late to the text revolution. My phone is not that fancy, so it is really hard to type on it. But also, I never get why people don't just call you and then get off quickly if the objective is a short message relayed.

I constantly battle with my students about the rudeness factor of texts. "But you weren't teaching just then!" Still! Just don't do it; I don't whip out my iPod and tune you out when you take tests. I sit there dutifully looking at you all as you scribble and sweat. Do the same, dang it.

But I do think they are really good for one thing: unobtrusively sending a message. Like, are you lying in bed when something suddenly occurs to you? Need to tell someone? Text it. They'll probably have their phone off anyway.

It's also good for noisy places. I'll give you that.

But not so good for trying to make your case to an ex.

So, anyway, I decide a text-reminder that I need some stuff at his house would be a nice way to approach it.

So off I go: "Hey, can I get my stuff back?"

Moments later: "Hi! I'm sorry I'm such a flake. I'll mail it by Wednesday."

Okay, cool.

Wednesday comes and goes. And the next one.

Me, via text: "No package."

An hour later . . . Him: "Yeah, I'm sorry. I'm writing a letter to you that I wanted to put in with it. I just mailed the package. I'll send the letter separately."

This coming from a guy who never once acknowledged one of mine? The sentiment is kind of sweet except when you consider that this guy has a longstanding history of being intensely selfish but convincing himself he's doing good: for example, holding on to stuff I *need*, so he can make himself feel better by writing me some letter.

And I ponder the contents of the letter. It can only be a few things:

A "I hope you rot in hell and here is all that's wrong with you" letter, but I know it's not this one. He's too good of a person at heart, and so am I. Nobody got the raw deal here.

A "I want you back, I miss you like hell" letter, which could be really flattering, but seeing as how he's independent and that's one thing I liked about him, I doubt it. Besides, then I would feel crummy, because I definitely don't want him back.

Or . . .

A "I still want to be best friends with you and call you when I have a bad day" letter.

All of the above really aren't going to do anything *for* me except make me agonize about how or whether to respond. The guy is clearly just doing it for his ego's sake - one way or another. This is the type of letter that should be written to make you feel better, and then burned.

The mystery (not much of one) is solved when I indignantly reply to his text: "Keep your letter; no good can come of it."

This takes me at least ten minutes to type out on my phone. I am not good at the text-fu. I might also add that it's coming to me on the side of a mountain I am attempting to run up. It is intensely hard to maintain pace when your ex is texting. He is, however, successful in keeping my heart rate elevated.

He writes back, almost instantly (because he has a BlackBerry or something like that with a QWERTY keyboard): "I can't believe you can't see the glass as half full."

I look at it, incredulously. I am so mad at this point. This was not a painful breakup for me. It had to happen, and right afterward, I felt so totally free and had such wonderful times with my friends that I was grateful it was over. But at the same time, the good times weren't lost on me, nor the things he taught me. The glass is totally half full. Oooh, I want to call him up and tell him so.

And as I am typing a reply, then backspacing, then typing, because I need to figure out how to get this across in a few lines with no context or tone imparted to them, I get this: "I can't believe you can do this. Fine. Enjoy your life. I hold no ill will and I'll be here when you come to your senses."

Ahh!!! My senses!!! Lots of people have clean breaks with their exes! I am not a freak. And yet, because I tend to like to rise to a challenge, I can't let it lie.

I have not moved from my spot on the trail. I am getting annoyed that my afternoon stroll with dog is going nowhere. So is the Fury

So, I weigh my options - what I can do and what I should do. At all costs, I don't need to flay this guy. He doesn't have to get the wallop. I just need him to quit inciting me. So I write back a sensible, "You are still being selfish, even if you don't see it. You didn't mail my stuff back because you didn't make it a priority, and then you held onto it so you could write a letter to me. That won't change a thing."

I find a place on a rock to sit and look out over the San Luis Obispo valley, waiting for my phone to chime.

He comes back with: "But you've so positively affected my life!" (This is his mantra, and I'm glad of it. It means I've been a success in my interactions with him, but that doesn't mean I owe him more.)

So I write: "I know I have. That's why I don't need the letter. I am glad the relationship is over. I'm happy."

And that's it. I hear nothing, so I merrily stuff my phone back in my pocket and head up to the summit.

I'm nearly to the top, when the phone chimes again, "Okay. Good. Have a good life."

And I'm kind of sad again. I don't like telling people to buzz off, even if it's better for all involved. But, I'm also giddy. I hate text drama. I just wasted forty minutes on maybe one hundred words.

Though, I like to imagine what it looked like on his end. I mean, here I am on a hillside in the afternoon on a hike. I'm gesticulating to no one like a mad man, making harrumph noises . . . all over a friggin' text.

But no, neither one of us is going to make that phone call. Too much.

And he let me go.

Or so I thought.

Four months later, I turned my phone on, and there it was, a text message: "Hi. I thought I'd give it a try again and ask you back into my life."

YAAAARGG! And by his doing this, I have to launch into a paroxysm of self evaluation. What do I want? Is it better to let him back or not? Am I a bitch for making either choice? What is the right thing to do?

I agonize over it for a day. I call some friends for advice. No one is very specific. Inner turmoil.

All over a damned text message.

Finally, after a week of looking at it, I made a choice and deleted it. When a friend followed up on my choice, I told him that a text was not exactly enough of a demonstration of this guy's worth.

"Well, what would he have to do?"

Luckily, I'd thought of this. Don't send me an unobtrusive text. Show up at my door. Have a real, live, sacked-up, non-cowardly conversation. Demonstrate that you understand my side of it and convince me I'm wrong. Convince me that I benefit from this relationship you're demanding, too.

But, Holy Maker on a Pancake, quit making me feel like a lout because of a stupid text message, which, by the way, cost me 10 cents.

Oh yeah, technology sure makes life easier.

EPILOGUE

I finished this book and sent it to publishers sometime in late December of 2008. I got some bites, but in the end it was a lot of rejection – I'd have to start a blog, have an established readership, there just wasn't a story line. The point of this is that there was no story line. There still isn't one.

That old adage of giving up and just not trying leading to the One turned out to be true for me. After I had sort of dated the guy I told you about in the introduction, the one whose story I promised not to write, I just quit trying.

Through most of my dating life, I had a best friend who was a guy, and also my business partner. He was cute, but non-threatening to the men I was trying out. He had a girlfriend. We were tight, but totally platonic, and I like to think that for his girlfriends, I too, was non-threatening. Maybe six months after I dated the last guy, my best friend's mom came to town and asked how the book was doing and how my dating life was going. I told her I'd given up on both. "Good," she said with relation to my dating, "That's how I met his father. I tried and tried and tried, and then it just worked out when I stopped."

A few months later, I was dating her son. We certainly never saw that happening.

He'd broken up with his girlfriend as they were going different places in life, and he started spending a lot more time with me. It was sort of annoying because he was *always* around. I loved him, but I wanted to go out on dates. He was offended if I socialized and didn't invite him. Over time, we started having dinner together every night. I had a girl friend of mine come to stay temporarily and she asked why I hadn't move on him. But, but, but . . . it's *him,* I said.

She pressed. Pointed out that we were so intimately involved with one another, we couldn't possibly give that intimacy to another person, at least not fully. This freaked me out. It took me a full month to process that. What it meant – what things would look like if I did or did not act on this knowledge. I had to think about the end-game. Could I have kids with this guy; heck, could I kiss him? Eww.

Eventually I got the guts to tell him that I'd been thinking about this stuff. He took a long time to respond, and then said, "I love you, but I'm not in love with you. I'm sorry. I think we should spend more time apart." Fine. His loss.

So I go about trying to spend more time apart. But what happens? He starts spending more time with me. People ask where he is if I don't bring him along, we're that tight.

We end up at a business conference for his business that I did marketing for, and long-story short, I'd been thinking about moving for a while and he kind of violated my trust at one point during the week. In a fury, I took the afternoon off and wandered around the city. I called my best friend and my father for counsel and decided it was time to move, no relationship in sight, a weird thing going with this guy who's my best friend and business partner, and kind of nothing in the way of money making on the horizon . . .

He met up with me later that night at a free concert I'd found and he asked me what was wrong. I told him.

No, more like gave it to him. There were tears on both our accounts, and it ended in a tearful hug, but for now at least there was peace. I was moving and the whole dilemma was finally resolved.

We flew back the next day, having an amazing time. We have a neat way of talking to each other that tends to amuse people around us, and this was one of those days that reminded me why I was so devoted to him.

When we got back, we went to check on the climbing gym that we were spending the summer building. There we were, standing in the drying stucco forest of climbing walls, when I look up and he grabs me from behind. I think ruefully, "There he goes flirting again." But this time it was different.

He spins me around and locks me into a kiss.

My knees buckled. It felt like it lasted forever. You know those cliché scenes in movies with a camera spinning around the couple and fireworks exploding? This was fireworks. There have never been fireworks before this.

And maybe it's not happily ever after (why don't they write songs about the realities of actually being in a serious relationship?), but I write this to you almost two years later and we're doing great. I have reason to believe I'll never have to write another bad dating story again.

So, yeah, kiss every frog you find. Even ones you've known forever. You never know which one will turn into that prince.

Kristin Tara McNamara

ABOUT THE AUTHOR

Kristin Tara McNamara is a part-time professor, part-time entrepreneur, and full-time entertainer. She loves her dogs, her family, her dude, and clearly, as this book shows, has self-esteem issues if she attracted dorkuses like she describes.

But we love her anyway.

www.ingramcontent.com/pod-product-compliance
Lightning Source LLC
Chambersburg PA
CBHW060938040426
42445CB00011B/915

9780615433097